Manmohanomics

Journey to South Block

(Life of an Indian Prime Minister)

A Portrait of Manmohan Singh

Manmohanomics

Journey to South Block

(Life of an Indian Prime Minister)

Vivek Garg

Ravish Mishra

Manas Publications

New Delhi - 110 002 (India)

MANAS PUBLICATIONS
(We Convert Fighters into Writers)
(Publishers for IAS, IPS, IFS, IRS, Defence, Press, Judges

4402/5-A, Ansari Road (Opp HDFC Bank)
Darya Ganj, New Delhi-110 002 (India)
Off.: 23260783, 23265523, Fax: 011-23272766
E-mail: manaspublications@gmail.com
manaspublications@yahoo.com

Third Impression 2013

ISBN: 81-7049-211-4

Rs. 495/-

Designed at
Manas Publications

Printed in India at
Rajdhani Printers, Delhi and published by Mrs Suman Lata for Manas Publications, 4402/5-A,
Ansari Road (Opp HDFC Bank),
Darya Ganj, New Delhi-110 002 (INDIA)

Preface

Journey to South Block

Dr. Manmohan Singh's journey that unexpectedly took him to the South Block in the New Delhi underscores the fact that he represents the very ethos of India.

It was a momentous day in the history of India when the Congress Party President, Mrs. Sonia Gandhi, decided not to be the Prime Minister of the country and nominated the economist with a magic wand, Dr. Manmohan Singh, to the most coveted office in the land.

Safe Hands

When Mrs. Gandhi and Dr. Singh emerged from the Rashtrapati Bhavan consequent to a meeting with the Indian President, Dr. APJ Abdul Kalam, to announce that Dr. Singh would be the Prime Minister, Mrs. Gandhi was virtually beaming with pleasure. So radiating was her presence when she said, "the country will be safe in Dr. Manmohan Singh's hands" that the gathered media persons asked the question, "Are you happy?" And her emphatic reply was, "Of course, I am very happy."

While Mrs. Gandhi admitted that a burden of responsibility had been shifted to Dr. Singh and she felt quite lighter in view of that, there was no hint of any tension in Dr. Singh's demeanour. The thorough professional that Dr. Singh is, he got straight down to business after taking oath as the Prime Minister of the country on 22 May 2004, spelling out the tasks that he had identified for his government and voiced his commitment to make good the promises made to the people.

Defining Moment

That was a defining moment when we decided to write a book on Dr. Manmohan Singh's journey that has taken him to South Block, the office of the Indian Prime Minister.

Since Dr. Singh's humility and simplicity is almost self-effacing, very little is known about his life, despite the fact that his achievements are stupendous. He kept a low profile while working at the highest levels in the Government of India. Consequently, for any book to do justice to Dr. Singh's persona, one had to dwell into whatever material was available, research what others have said about him, and then mould the material into a story as remarkable as the life of Dr. Manmohan Singh.

That defining moment in the forecourt of the Rashtrapati Bhavan when the simple Sikh donning his trademark sky-blue turban and flowing kurta-pyjama accepted charge of the country, the formal oath taking coming a few days later, also began an educative and rewarding journey for us.

We sifted through material on Dr. Singh's birthplace in the village of Gah, 50 miles from the Pakistani capital, Islamabad, to his early education in Amritsar. His matriculation, inter, graduation and post-graduation from the Punjab University, to his higher studies in Cambridge and Oxford.

The picture became clear of a man with rare determination and perseverance, a person with a humble background striving to excel by dint of sheer hard work, an individual gifted with great intellectual merit and an innate wisdom.

Original Thinker

Above all, the material on this period of Dr. Singh's life gave an insight into a fine human being whose honesty of purpose was unshakable, whose vision was grounded in unadulterated patriotism and one who dared to sift the corn of knowledge from the chaff. An original thinker, Dr. Manmohan Singh had the courage to think on lines other than conventional wisdom and to seek the truth even as he pursued academic excellence.

We looked at Dr. Singh's consequent stint abroad with UNCTAD, the love for the country then bringing him back to India, and the spirit to do something for his own country with the tools of knowledge that he had acquired.

We studied Dr. Singh's seven-year teaching stint at the Punjab University, which showed steady progress to higher ranks. And, his shorter duration with the Delhi School of Economics; in both places his keen insight endearing him to his colleagues and his students alike.

Then came Dr. Singh's twenty years with the Government of India in the capacity of an economic administrator. Looking at this period of Dr. Singh's illustrious career, one espies some traces of restlessness. He did not hold one position for very long and quickly moved to another posting. Being constantly on the move from one challenging task to the other, Dr. Singh must have got both a macro- and the micro-view of the functioning of the Government of India, which would be a great advantage in finding remedies to the ills that afflict the babudom, that is the face of the Government of India.

New Role

Finally, Dr. Singh was handpicked by Prime Minister Narasimha Rao to be his Finance Minister in 1991, and with that began a completely new role for Dr. Singh, which ultimately landed him in the South Block in just 13 short years. With his very original economic policies, Dr. Singh proceeded to free the ordinary Indian from the clutches of the licence-quota-permit raj and within a couple of years put the Indian economy on the track of rapid growth. His five-year Finance Ministership clearly gave Dr. Singh the opportunity to test his own original ideas and theories that he must have developed while studying economics at the world's renowned centres of knowledge, or as a government servant. It must have been extremely pleasing for coming up trumps with his long-held theories, despite the varying views held by many others. Dr. Singh's panacea of freedom and opportunity for the Indian entrepreneur worked wonders. He was truly a man with a magic wand for the Indian economy.

Going through the available material on Dr. Singh's life, one is forced to draw the conclusion that he is just an ordinary Indian at heart whom destiny has made the Prime Minister of the country in view of his academic merit, intellectual prowess, sheer achievements and because his heart beats for India.

Dr. Singh has all the traits of an average Indian. He is sincere and hardworking. He is talented and honest. He is uncompromisingly patriotic. He is not a seeker, but a giver. He believes in God and in the theory that one should do one's duty without thinking of the rewards. Above all, he has compassion in his heart, and empathy.

An Inspiring Figure

So, what is so special about Manmohan Singh? Perhaps, the fact that he has the determination to go that extra last mile to achieve his target. He has the staying power to keep trying and not to give up. He has the inner strength not to give up in the face of adversity, not to panic in a difficult situation, the resolve to be unrelenting, faith in God and confidence in the talent and ingenuity of the Indian people. This makes Dr. Manmohan Singh a figure that inspires with his unflappable calm. A leader who exudes confidence that everything is under control.

As Finance Minister, Dr. Manmohan Singh worked wonders with his original ideas in the field of economics. Dr. Singh has also been a keen student of politics, cultures and civilizations. He has original ideas on these subjects too. If morning shows the day, Prime Minister Singh should move the country in the direction of better politics and a better society in the days to come. And, as a role model, he can spark changes for the better in millions of lives of ordinary Indians with humble beginnings like him.

Writing this book on the life of Dr. Manmohan Singh has been as rewarding as it has been inspiring. The success story that Dr. Singh's life is, stands testimony to the merit and relevance of the very concept of India and all the values that this great civilization stands for.

Vivek Garg
Ravish Mishra

Contents

PM-designate showing the letter he received from the President

The Former President, Shri R. Venkataraman administering the oath of office of Cabinet Minister, to Dr. Manmohan Singh in New Delhi on June 21, 1991

Prime Minister Manmohan Singh is greeted by Congress President Sonia Gandhi and senior CPM leader Somnath Chatterjee after he was sworn-in on May 22, 2004

Dr. Manmohan Singh paying a courtesy call on A.B. Vajpayee

PM Dr. Manmohan Singh - Taking Charge at South Block

CHAPTER

1

Crown of Thorns for the Dark Horse

It was an unprecedented and bizarre sequence of events stretching over a full week. Mercifully, it culminated in the announcement on May 18, 2004, by the Congress Party President, Mrs. Sonia Gandhi, that Dr. Manmohan Singh would be the next Prime Minister of India.

Implicit Trust

A relaxed and smiling Mrs. Sonia Gandhi also voiced her conviction that "the country will be safe in Dr. Manmohan Singh's hands." Clearly, Dr. Singh enjoyed Mrs. Gandhi's implicit trust and faith.

There had been so many twists and turns of events and circumstances ever since the trends and results of the Lok

Sabha elections started coming in on the morning of May 13, that no one could have had any inkling that Dr. Manmohan Singh would indeed assume the most powerful job in the country.

For one, the verdict of the Indian voter was not clearly in any one party's favour, though the Congress Party did emerge as the one with the highest number of Lok Sabha members. The Bharatiya Janata Party came a very close second.

Crucial Role of Communists

Even the pre-poll alliance forged by Mrs. Sonia Gandhi's Congress Party with such allies as Laloo Prasad Yadav's Rashtriya Janata Dal and Ram Vilas Paswan's Lok Janshakti Party in Bihar, Dr. Karunanidhi's Dravida Munnetra Kazhagham and its clutch of associates in Tamil Nadu, Mr. Chandrashekhar Rao's Telangana Rashtriya Samiti (TRS) in Andhra Pradesh, Sharad Pawar's Nationalist Congress Party in Maharashtra, the Jharkhand Mukti Morcha etc., fell short of a Lok Sabha majority of 272 seats in a House of 542, by some fifty seats.

It was the extension of support by the 60-plus-member grouping of the Left Parties (the Communist Party of India (Marxist), the Communist Party of India, the Forward Bloc and the RSP) to the Congress Party and its pre-poll allies that made this Congress-Communist combine a clear winner. Given this situation, it was only a matter of time for Mulayam Singh Yadav's Samajwadi Party, Mr. Ajit Singh's Rashtriya Lok Dal and Ms. Mayawati's Bahujan Samaj Party to resort to some pragmatic politics and extend support to this combine.

The snowballing support meant that there were more than 310 elected Lok Sabha members supporting Mrs. Sonia Gandhi's Prime Ministerial bid, in a House of 542 members. It took a couple of days of hectic negotiations and parleys between the Congress and the Communists for this winning combine to be forged, and Dr. Manmohan Singh's name figured nowhere in the reckoning for the post of Prime Minister.

The Dark Horse

The rank and file of the Congress Party, in their enthusiasm, interpreted the verdict as the people's mandate for Mrs. Sonia Gandhi to be the Prime Minister of the country, which is the biggest democracy on earth.

The Congress Party pursued this direction, and the delirious Congress Party leaders unanimously elected her the leader of the Congress Parliamentary Party, making her the automatic choice to be Prime Minister. Who knew then, that Dr. Manmohan Singh was the dark horse, who would ultimately emerge as Sonia Gandhi's nominee for the top-job in India?

All the allies of the Congress Party like the Maharashtra strongman Mr. Sharad Pawar and Dr. Karunanidhi from Tamil Nadu pressed Sonia to be Prime Minister, and even Communist stalwarts like Comrades Jyoti Basu and Harkishen Singh Surjit supported her premiership.

It was at that point of time, when the Prime Minister's office was in her lap, that Sonia Gandhi declined to be Prime Minister, citing her "inner voice" as the reason for her decision, and finally named Dr. Manmohan Singh as her choice for being India's Prime Minister.

In the Congress Party, Sonia Gandhi's word is law. If she wished Dr. Manmohan Singh to be the Prime Minister, no one could say no. Most Congress leaders took the line of imploring and beseeching Sonia Gandhi to change her mind and not to be deterred from accepting the office of Prime Minister. But all the pleading was to no avail, and the self-effacing Dr. Manmohan Singh, who describes himself as a "professor and a civil servant" accompanied Mrs. Gandhi to the Rashtrapati Bhavan, where he staked his claim before the President, Dr. APJ Abdul Kalam, and was in turn invited to take oath as the Prime Minister.

Not a Politician

It will be safe to say without any fear of contradiction that Dr. Manmohan Singh is not the average Indian politician who will do anything for popularity. In fact, when Dr. Manmohan Singh contested an election for the Lok Sabha in 1998, from the sophisticated South Delhi constituency, he lost at the hands of Bharatiya Janata Party's Prof. Vijay Kumar Malhotra. It is indeed creditworthy for the academic to be a misfit in the hurly-burly of electoral politics.

Dr. Manmohan Singh is a man of integrity and there is no charge of scandal or scam involving him. It may be noted that the worst ever scam of the Indian stock markets took place in the early 1990s when Dr. Manmohan Singh was India's Finance Minister. That was the time that the big bull Harshad Mehta took the Bombay Sensex to dizzying heights and the crash thereafter financially ruined lakhs of small investors. However, so spotlessly clean has been the career of Dr. Singh as a professor, as a civil servant and as a politician that no finger was pointed at him.

A Decent Man

Dr. Manmohan Singh lives the life of a decent, ordinary man. His colleagues point out that this much-accomplished person keeps an old Maruti-800, the people's car in India, whereas very junior people would be driving flashier and bigger vehicles. Dr. Singh drives this car himself, rather than keeping a driver, say those who know him well.

Dr. Manmohan Singh is known as the architect of India's economic reforms. As the Finance Minister of the country in the Congress Party government of Mr. P V Narasimha Rao from 1991 to 1996, he initiated the process of unshackling the Indian economy from the vice-like grip of the licence-quota-permit raj. The economic reforms that he initiated have lifted the country from dire economic straits to the threshold of becoming an economic powerhouse.

Even the Narasimha Rao government did not enjoy a majority in the Lok Sabha. It was dependent on outside support for its survival. It is to the credit of Dr. Manmohan Singh that he fashioned economic reforms in such a way as to win all-round approval and pursued a new path without jeopardizing the survival of the Rao government.

Today's Manmohan Singh government would be entirely dependent on the 60-plus-member support of the Communist parties for its very survival. It will be the Left Front that will be dictating policy and vetoing any policy measures that are not to their liking. It will, thus, require all the ingenuity at Dr. Manmohan Singh's command to carry forward economic reforms with the support of the Communists.

An inkling of how things can go sour can be had in the mayhem in the Indian stock markets a few days after the election results when some Communist Party leaders said on television that the disinvestment ministry must be scrapped and that the stock markets do not reflect the health of the Indian economy.

Reassuring Presence

When the stock markets opened for trading on the day following these statements, it took only a few minutes for the Sensex to fall ten percent, for the circuit breaker to be hit and for trading to be stopped. After the cooling period, it again took only a few minutes for the indices to shed five more percent and for the second circuit breaker to be hit and trading to be stopped. It was then that Dr. Manmohan Singh appeared on television, reassured the investors about his commitment to economic reforms and to policies that are investment friendly. He had a talk with the Finance Minister, Mr. Jaswant Singh, and ensured liquidity in the share market. When the markets reopened, they regained much of the lost ground.

Dr. Manmohan Singh recognizes that a healthy stock market is important for the growth of the Indian economy. However, he will need to use all his tact to curb the natural inclination of various leaders of the Communist Parties to make such statements.

"Economic Reforms with a Human Face", is the mantra that Dr. Manmohan Singh has been espousing of late, the "Human Face" being in deference to the verdict of the electorate. Explaining this, Dr. Singh says that economic reforms should not benefit just a few but also be of direct benefit to the poor. Linking economic reforms to employment-generation seems to be his priority even as he speaks out against "jobless growth". Yes, Dr. Manmohan Singh's latest balancing act is designed to keep the Communists happy even as the economic reforms continue with a few modifications.

The Cramping CMP

The Common Minimum Programme or "CMP" created as the guideline for the functioning of the Manmohan Singh government is the instrument that should keep all the supporting parties on board, and also keep the government from straying in matters of policy.

While the DMK has made abundantly clear its opposition to the Prevention of Terrorism Act (POTA), the Communist parties have spoken out against disinvestment of profit-making public sector corporations and against the "hire-and-fire policy" regarding labour. Rashtriya Janata Dal's Laloo Yadav wants an economic package for his Bihar state while the TRS wants a separate state of Telangana carved out of Andhra Pradesh. Ram Vilas Paswan wants subsidies to the Indian farmer to continue. Dr. Manmohan Singh must come to grips with these and similar demands as he pursues the policy of economic reforms.

While the reason cited by Mrs. Sonia Gandhi for not accepting the job of the Prime Minister of India, which was hers for the taking, has been her "inner voice" telling her not to do it, there is quite some speculation about what could be the other factors prompting Sonia's decision, which gave the Prime Minister's chair to Dr. Manmohan Singh.

Rumour

Comrade Jyoti Basu has said that it could be Sonia's children, Rahul and Priyanka, who have seen the tragic killings of their father (Rajiv Gandhi) and grandmother (Mrs. Indira Gandhi), who dissuaded her from becoming Prime Minister, lest they lose her too. But this could only be a rumour that Basu was referring to.

Then there was this "nationwide movement" that BJP leaders were threatening to launch on the issue of Sonia Gandhi being of Italian origin, if she was sworn in as Prime Minister. BJP's firebrand leader, Ms. Sushma Swaraj, said that she would shave her head, wear white clothes, and sleep on the floor so long as Sonia remained Prime Minister.

Madhya Pradesh's BJP Chief Minister, Ms. Uma Bharti, threatened resignation and called Mrs. Gandhi becoming Prime Minister a "national shame". Even BJP's Govindacharya came out of oblivion and took up the issue of Soni'a being of foreign origin. Could it be that Sonia Gandhi stepped aside to deprive the BJP of this potent rallying issue?

The Lok Sabha election results deflated the BJP. Mr. Atal Behari Vajpayee went completely quiet. Perhaps, Mrs. Sonia Gandhi did not wish to give any handle to the BJP that could spur the party's revival.

Inner Voice

It may be recalled that on an earlier occasion, in 1998, Mrs. Sonia Gandhi had gone to the Rashtrapati Bhawan to stake her claim to be Prime Minister, after the government of Atal Behari Vajpayee fell on the floor of the Lok Sabha, being shy by one vote. It was allegedly the non-cooperation of the Samajwadi Party that put a spanner in the works then and kept Mrs. Sonia Gandhi from being Prime Minister.

Could it be that Mrs. Gandhi did not wish to be Prime Minister of a government that would be at the mercy of other parties? After all, the Congress Party would be only one partner, albeit the leading one, among several partners in the Manmohan Singh government. Incidentally, Mr. Rajiv Gandhi had preferred to sit in the opposition on an earlier occasion when the Congress Party had won thirty more seats than it has won in 2004.

In any case, Mrs. Sonia Gandhi remains the Chairperson of the Congress Parliamentary Party as also the President of the Congress Party. Dr. Manmohan Singh is a staunch and loyal follower who would be consulting Mrs. Gandhi at every step. With him as Prime Minister, Mrs. Sonia Gandhi and her Congress Party would not fear of an alternative centre of power emerging, at least in the near future.

What bearing would all this have on the longevity of the Manmohan Singh government? It is not a widely held view that this government would last its full term. Many analysts give it about a year-and-a-half at the least and three years at most.

In the year 2006, state assembly elections are due in the states of the Tamil Nadu, Maharashtra, and more notably, in West Bengal and Kerala. So, a year and a half from now, politics in New Delhi could be dictated by the demands of the forthcoming assembly elections.

Communists' Dilemma

In West Bengal and Kerala, the Communist Parties are directly pitted against the Congress Party in a two-way electoral battle. Actually, the bulk of the highest-ever 60-plus seats that the Communists have won in the 2004 Lok Sabha polls have been in these two states, after a bitter campaign against the Congress Party. The BJP is virtually insignificant in these two states. If the Communists will be seen as supporters of the Congress Party government in New Delhi, how will they oppose the same party in the assembly elections in West Bengal and Kerala with any degree of conviction? Will this double-speak not provide the BJP a firmer foothold in these two states?

This fear is one reason why the Communists have opted out of the Manmohan Singh government and prefer to support it from outside. Actually, it would be in the interest of the Communists to be critical of the Congress Party's policies, so as to get some dividends in the West Bengal and Kerala assembly elections.

This political truth makes it very difficult for the Communists to support Dr. Manmohan Singh's economic reform agenda, especially when it flies in the face of all that the communists stand for as regards labour protection and private profit. Communists' criticism of Dr. Manmohan Singh's policies should get shriller as the state assembly season draws nearer.

Though the Tamil Nadu and Maharashtra assembly elections may not throw up such a contradiction, they would remain a test of popularity and entail keeping Sharad Pawar's NCP and Karunanidhi's DMK in good humour.

Striking a Balance

Given this situation, the budgets presented by the Manmohan Singh government in Parliament must incorporate a balance of the Congress Party's Vision and that of the allies. Financial whizkid though the new Finance Minister Mr. P Chidambaram is, he will need to be a financial acrobat to keep all sides happy.

Thus, the Manmohan Singh government will have to think on its feet to survive and it is to be seen how long it lasts. Dr. Manmohan Singh is not known as an astute politician. He is a man who neither takes nor gives favours. What chance would he have to reconcile the Laloos and Surjits, the Pawars and Karunanidhis?

However, there is also the view that the Dr. Manmohan Singh of the year 2004 is more political savvy than the political novice of 1991, when he first became Finance Minister.

Perhaps, Mrs. Sonia Gandhi may have chosen Manmohan Singh precisely because he looks like a political novice, dependent on others even to get into Parliament. He has no large following or power base that can be a political threat. He will do what he is told to do. He is extremely loyal and can be relied upon not to play political games. That makes him the dark horse, surging ahead of real time politicians like Congress Party stalwarts like Arjun Singh and Pranab Mukherjee to become the Prime Minister of the country.

Good Economics is Good Politics

The ascendancy of Dr. Manmohan Singh to the Prime Minister's post is also reflective of the changing nature of

Indian politics. Roads, electricity, drinking water, infrastructure, bread and butter have all become election issues now, and decide who will win the polls and who will be consigned to the dustbin. Emotive issues are not enough by themselves to win elections. Non-performance on the economic front creates the anti-incumbency factor that plays havoc with a ruling party that goes into an election. Parties need a Manmohan Singh who may not be politically savvy but can deliver growth with welfare through astute economic policies.

It may be noted that the Manmohan Singh government may not have too much time in which to deliver. A couple of years is not enough time to show results but is sufficient time for anti-incumbency to set in. Dr. Manmohan Singh's government would be presenting two budgets in these two years, which would be his instruments for ushering change and delivering results.

Dr. Manmohan Singh's becoming the Prime Minister of India has quite some political significance to. Born on September 26, 1932 in Gah in West Punjab (now in Pakistan), he hails from the Sikh community and initially had his education at the University of Punjab after which he went on to the Universities of Cambridge and Oxford for pursuing higher studies. That makes him a highly educated and respected Sikh from the pre-partition West Punjab.

Endearing the Sikh Community

It is widely believed that ever since the 1984 anti-Sikh riots following Mrs. Indira Gandhi's assassination in Delhi and other cities of North India in which more than 2000 Sikhs are believed to have been killed, this community started voting against the Congress Party. Before 1984, it is believed that the Sikhs were supporters of the Congress Party.

When Mrs. Sonia Gandhi nominated Dr. Manmohan Singh to be the Prime Minister, many believed that this brought the Sikh community closer to the Congress Party, and perhaps, to the Gandhi family. After all it is during Mrs. Indira Gandhi's time that Giani Zail Singh, a Sikh from an average background, became the President of the country, and now Mrs. Sonia Gandhi has nominated this unassuming Sikh named Dr. Manmohan Singh as the Prime Minister, by making way for him.

The support of the Sikh community can be the incremental support for the Congress Party that can make the difference on a score of seats to the Lok Sabha, restoring some of the erstwhile stature that the Congress Party has lost in recent years.

Challenging Task

Politics notwithstanding, it will be on the touchstone of "economic growth with employment" and "reforms with a human face" that Dr. Manmohan Singh will be judged. The good doctor will have to come up with some effective remedies, and fast, to create public support, in the process proving that he is no political light-weight after all.

Here it must be said that it is the situation that brings forth the man. After the death of Pandit Jawaharlal Nehru in 1964, the Congress Party was led by the then unassuming dark horse Lal Bahadur Shastri, who was considered a faceless political light-weight. Shastri is credited with initiating the Green Revolution to make Indian agriculture self-sufficient. He also won a resounding victory for India in the 1965 Indo-Pak war. The two-year Shastri legacy is still an asset for the Congress Party, even though this self-effacing man with a humble background did not hail from the Nehru-Gandhi family.

It is to be seen if Prime Minister Manmohan Singh, who is not from the Nehru-Gandhi family, can do for the country something similar to what Lal Bahadur Shastri did by galvanizing the nation with the battle cry of *"Jai Jawan Jai Kisan"*.

Dr. Manmohan Singh has been catapulted into the prime minister's office by a bizarre sequence of events that no one could have foreseen. He has an appeal that cuts across party lines. It is to be seen what destiny and the quirk of circumstances are conjuring up for Prime Minister Manmohan Singh, whose assuming office certainly marks a new era in Indian politics.

Top: Manmohan with his brothers(from right)
Daljit Singh, Surinder Singh(deceased) and Surjit Singh
Centre: Brother Daljit and Surjit celebrating his brother's becoming PM
Bottom: Pritan Kaur, younger sister(third from left) of Dr. Manmohan Singh, and her family celebrating at their residence in Kolkata

Top: Manmohan Singh's father Gurmukh Singh Kohli and mother Krishna Kaur
Centre: Manmohan Singh with his wife Gursharan Kaur
Bottom: Dr. Manmohan Singh at the wedding of Surjit Singh in 1982

CHAPTER

2

Humble Beginning in Gah, (now in Pakistan)

It was on September 26, 1932, that Manmohan Singh was born in the Gah village of West Punjab. Even today, despite being a mere fifty miles south-west of the Pakistani capital city of Islamabad, Gah seems to be like what it was 70 years ago, steeped in abject poverty and largely untouched by modernization.

Charpoys Under Neem Trees

Gah is an assortment of *kutcha* and *semi-pucca* small houses. Cows and buffaloes graze about, and the agricultural folks sit on charpoys under neem trees, sweating profusely in the hot and humid weather. Poverty is writ large on the lined, weather-beaten faces of the residents of Gah. Women still carry water in earthen pitchers balanced on their heads and thus take it to their houses, manually fetching it from wells.

The highway from Islamabad is a few miles from Gah, and there is no motorable road from it to the village of Manmohan Singh's birth, reflecting the lack of development even in the vicinity of the Pakistani capital. There are plenty of villages in India that are not approachable by road, but perhaps not within a fifty-mile radius of New Delhi.

However, Gah does have intermittent electricity supply, satellite television and even the odd tractor.

Little "Mohna" Remembered

Gah's village school, called the government primary school, is ramshackle though spacious and old men recall that Manmohan studied in this very school as their class-fellow. "I failed and Manmohan passed," recalls Mohammad Ashraf, sitting on a cot under a tree. But Ashraf does not know the Indian Prime Minister as Manmohan Singh. It was only when the name of Gurmukh Singh Kohli (Manmohan's father) was taken that 70-year-old Ashraf's face reportedly lit up and broke into a grin as he remembered "Little Mohna".

When Manmohan Singh was raised in this village, half the village's population was Hindu or Sikh, and the other half was Muslim. Today, the entire population of this village is Muslim. But this demographic change is not of the villagers' making. The flight of the Hindus and the Sikhs from Gah to India after partition in 1947 was due to the riots that broke out all over, despite the fact that all communities lived in peace, cooperation and friendship in this village.

He Has Done Gah Proud

Other Gah villagers including Abdul Khaliq and Raja Gulsher are very proud that a man who was born in their village has become the Prime Minister of a great democracy called India. "We are very proud that a child of this village, who studied in this village school, has become the Prime Minister of India. We expect that this will be very auspicious for furthering friendship between our two countries."

Manmohan Singh's father, Gurmukh Singh Kohli, and mother, Amrit Kaur, would call him "Mohna" when he was a child, and that was the name that the present Indian Prime Minister was known by in Gah. Manmohan Singh grew up in Gah way back in the 1930s but the villagers are so happy at the achievement of this son-of-their-soil that the Indian Prime Minister has a standing invitation to visit the village of his birth where a tumultuous welcome awaits him.

His origin in Gah places Manmohan Singh in a uniquely advantageous position to carry forward the ongoing India-Pakistan effort to forge friendly relations. He speaks that dialect of the Punjabi language that is spoken in the heart of Pakistan, and he also understands the nuances of the spoken words and responses.

It is interesting that while Dr. Manmohan Singh was born 71 summers ago in a village near the Pakistani capital city, the Pakistani leader, General Parvez Musharraf, was born in the Indian capital city of New Delhi. Surely, they would understand each other's country like the back of their hands and would have an emotional attachment to their place of birth like any other human being.

Experiences of Partition

On the other hand, the experiences of these two leaders would also include the pangs of the partition of the Indian sub-continent when it became free of British rule in 1947. Those experiences would not be happy ones for either leader. Hundreds of thousands of Hindus, Sikhs and Muslims were killed in the communal carnage that followed the partition of the subcontinent. It is inexplicable why the retreating British partitioned this sub-continent into India and Pakistan purely on communal grounds resulting in an unparalleled human tragedy.

Manmohan Singh's father was a dry fruit merchant and was fortunate to have moved to Amritsar, the holiest city of Sikhs, a few years before the partition. So, his family did not personally flee Gah after partition. But since Amritsar was the entry point into India for the Hindu and Sikh "Refugees" who were fleeing Pakistan through the Wagah border or came by train from adjacent Lahore, Manmohan Singh's family would not be untouched by the aftermath of partition.

If both Manmohan Singh and Pervez Musharraf have drawn appropriate lessons from the catastrophic communal riots some 60 years ago, in which large numbers of their compatriots perished, they would certainly make efforts to write a new, happier chapter in India-Pakistan ties based on the pre-partition halcyon days in Gah and in Shahjahanabad, the latter being that part of the Walled City of Delhi where President Musharraf grew up.

In the coming days and months, Manmohan and Musharraf would be dealing with each other in an attempt to put the frosty past in India-Pakistan relations behind and to write a new chapter of cooperation and even a partnership that can take South Asia forward.

Forging Peace With Pakistan

Even before he had taken oath of office, Dr Manmohan Singh pledged to work with General Musharraf to forge ties of peace, friendship and cooperation between India and Pakistan.

It may be noted that Dr. Manmohan Singh has emerged as the Prime Minister of a so-called "Secular" front that has been spearheaded by the Congress Party. This front has pledged to fight what they call "communal" forces in Indian polity.

Those who know Dr. Manmohan Singh say that it is this humble beginning and schooling in Gah that provides the Indian Prime Minister with the experience and insight to empathize with the poverty and lack of opportunity which vast multitudes in both India and Pakistan grapple with on a daily basis.

"Manmohan Singh has not read about poverty in some book. He has experienced it at first hand. So he can understand the challenges that the poor people face and can find solutions that work", say his associates, referring to his humble beginning in Gah.

That explains Dr. Manmohan Singh's immediate focus on carrying forward the ongoing process of economic reforms in India, but with a human face. He abhors programmes that cause disruption in the lives of the poor in the name of economic reforms. He wishes to link economic reforms with reaching the benefits of reforms to the deprived, and to make growth job-oriented and not jobless.

Lifting Agriculture from Stagnation

Agricultural stagnation prevalent in India pains Dr. Manmohan Singh, and he wishes to link economic reforms to a fillip in the agricultural sector. Despite all the growth in other sectors, India still remains largely an agricultural economy and Dr. Manmohan Singh realizes that India cannot be growing if Indian agriculture continues to stagnate.

Dr. Manmohan Singh is an advocate of the Mixed Economy. He says that India needs a vibrant private sector and also needs a healthy public sector. He is of the view that strategic enterprises like Gas Authority of India (GAIL) and the Oil and Natural Gas Corporation (ONGC) are required to be in the public sector and there is no need to privatize them. However, as public sector units, these enterprises would be free to tap the capital market.

Dr. Manmohan Singh is inspired by the prophecy of the Late Prime Minister, Mr. Rajiv Gandhi, that the 21st century will be India's century. Dr. Singh is determined to create the appropriate environment to make this possible.

After Gah, Dr. Manmohan Singh went on to study in Amritsar, and then pursued higher studies in Economics at the Universities of Oxford and of Cambridge. It appears that his first-hand experiences in Gah have provided Manmohan Singh the grounding that has given meaning to his later training as an Economic Administrator.

Manmohan's Gah-Advantage

Gah has clearly shaped and moulded Dr. Manmohan Singh in his formative years. He is positioned to succeed in bringing about a breakthrough in India-Pakistan relations. This soft-spoken, genial Sikh from Gah may well write a new chapter in economic cooperation in the Indian sub-continent that would benefit all countries in the region in addressing common challenges of poverty alleviation and of giving a better deal to their citizens.

Many Faces of Manmohan Singh

CHAPTER

3

Manmohan's Simple Private Life

Dr. Manmohan Singh is the first Sikh Prime Minister of India, which is happy news for the 25 million Sikhs worldwide. He embodies the Sikh virtues of hard work, sharing, caring, humility, honesty and simplicity, as also pride and the courage of conviction.

Squeaky Clean

What is more, Singh is squeaky clean and no corruption charge has ever been leveled at him despite his being in politics for 13 years. This is something rare in Indian politics where making a charge, substantiated or unsubstantiated, is the done thing by political adversaries.

Dr. Singh represents the state of Assam in the Upper House (Rajya Sabha) of India's bicameral Parliament, also called the House of Elders. It seems decent, squeaky clean and upright people who stand by their principles find it difficult to get elected to the Lower House of India's Parliament (Lok Sabha) also called the House of the People.

Saikias' Tenant

It was the then Assam Chief Minister, Mr. Hiteswar Saikia, who was instrumental in getting Singh elected to the Rajya Sabha from Assam in the early-1990s, for which a sufficient number of Assam Assembly members had to vote for Singh. When the Election Commission objected that Singh also had to be a resident of Assam, Saikia made Singh a tenant in his own house in Sarumataria, Guwahati, (the capital of the Assam State of India) where a wooden name-plate reading "M M Singh" has been adorning the door since the early-1990s.

Singh pays a monthly rental to the Saikias. After the death of Hiteswar Saikia, the strongman of the visionary North-east, this rental is being paid to his widow, Hemo Prava Saikia, who is a Minister in the Congress government in the state.

Hemo Prava Saikia says that Manmohan Singh "will never compromise on his principles."

House Number 3989, Nandan Nagar, Ward 51, Sarumataria, Dispur, Guwahati, remains the permanent address of Dr. Manmohan Singh.

A good deed always begets one in return. The Saikias had stood by Singh in getting him into the Rajya Sabha. However, since the death of Hiteswar Saikia almost a decade ago, his family was relegated to the background in intra-Congress politics so much so that there was even talk that Hemo Prava Saikia may be dropped from the Assam Council of Ministers to reduce the size of the Ministry. And, now that her tenant of thirteen years becomes the Prime Minister of the country the Assam Congress Party once again throngs to the Saikias.

A "Good Man"

Dr. Manmohan Singh's becoming the Prime Minister is being welcomed not just in the Punjab and in Assam and the North-east, but all over the country because he is described as a "good man". It is recalled on the street that he had pulled the country out of dire economic straits in the early 1990s and would once again improve the economic lot of the countrymen.

At the prestigious Delhi School of Economics in the north campus of the University of Delhi, there is an air of elation at Singh becoming the Prime Minister. The academic community sees in this the recognition of the role that the teaching community plays in nation-building. Singh taught International Trade at the Delhi School of Economics before he became an Economic Administrator.

The Ratan Tata Library at the Delhi School of Economics is among the best social sciences libraries. However, in the early 1990s this library was so strapped for funds that it could not even subscribe to journals. Dr. Manmohan Singh, the then Finance Minister of the country, was petitioned and he is supposed to have taken personal interest in the effort to bring this library back to financial health.

Academicians are especially happy that Dr. Manmohan Singh as Finance Minister had cut through red tape and the bureaucracy to deliver growth and welfare.

Increasing the tax to GDP ratio from the present 15 percent to a desired 18 percent is seen as one challenge before Prime Minister Manmohan Singh.

It is not that Prime Minister Manmohan Singh is all academics and no play. He is quite fond of sports, and used to love a game of volleyball, say his associates.

As soon as it became clear that Manmohan Singh would be the next Prime Minister of India, his house at 18 Safdarjung Road in New Delhi was virtually taken over by the highest level of security, including the commandos of the Special Protection Group (SPG). The house inside was a picture of middle-class simplicity, while outside the security, metal detectors, barricades etc., made it clear that the stature of the man inside the house was no ordinary one.

A Private Person

Dr. Singh is a man who keeps his personal life away from his public life, the former being his private affair. It is to be seen if he is able to continue this arrangement once he becomes Prime Minister and the media focuses on his every waking moment.

Dr. Manmohan Singh's eldest daughter, Upinder Singh, is the Head of the History Department at the prestigious

St. Stephen's College in Delhi. She is the author of the book *Ancient Delhi*. She has told the media that her father is a "man of few words". She has found him "thoughtful" and "absorbed in his own mind". He has allowed his three daughters to "make their own decisions" for which they admire him.

Dr. Manmohan Singh's life is a picture of simplicity and hard work and is exemplified by self-discipline. He is up and about at 6 in the morning, reads the papers, and is ready for work.

Gursharan, Source of Strength

Dr. Singh's wife, Gursharan, is described as his "quiet partner". Gursharan stands like a rock with her husband who is so engrossed in his work that he is able to give less time to the family. She loves cooking and being with the grandchildren. She is credited with putting Dr. Manmohan Singh's life in order. She is Manmohan Singh's inspiration and his source of strength. Is she the real power behind the "Man"?

Dr. Manmohan Singh does not go in for fancy food and prefers the simple *dal*, *subji* and *roti*, the very Indian meal. He is not too fond of meat.

Dr. Singh has held very important positions throughout his public life, but has always maintained a balance between his professional and personal life. He has never allowed success to go to his head.

Dr. Manmohan Singh's second daughter, Daman, has studied environment as a subject and works with a non-governmental organization, while the youngest one, Amrit, is a lawyer in New York. Amrit is the only one who studied economics.

Uncompromisingly Honest

Those who know him say that Dr. Manmohan Singh never gets impatient. He is uncompromising in his intellectual honesty.

India's great economist Amartya Sen recalls that Dr. Manmohan Singh was two years his junior when they were studying in Cambridge. And, there were celebrations in Cambridge too at Dr. Manmohan Singh's elevation to the top post in India.

Wearing a Crown of Thorns

Prime Minister Manmohan Singh - Humility Despite Towering Achievements

CHAPTER

4

Karmayogi* Par Excellence

The Indian Prime Minister, Dr. Manmohan Singh, is widely recognized as one among the world's leading economists. His distinguished career has been devoted to practical application of developmental economics.

Dr. Singh not only has a sterling academic career, he has a wealth of experience in international developmental organizations and in economic diplomacy. He has played crucial roles for more than two decades in framing and implementing India's economic policies and even in overseeing the planning process.

It is a sign of his sheer worth that this academic and economic administrator was handpicked to be India's Finance Minister in the year 1991 when the country's

* Karmayogi means `one who worship work'

foreign exchange reserves were negligible and there was danger of the country defaulting on its foreign loan instalments. The process of economic reforms that Dr. Singh then set in motion continued to reap the country rich dividends and enabled it to emerge as a strong economic force on the world stage.

Brilliant Mind

Dr. Singh's career can be divided into four distinct segments. His stint in academics at the Punjab University and at the Delhi School of Economics being the first. In a sense, this was an extension of Dr. Singh's education, as this brilliant mind dwelt on what course his life should take.

His short innings with the UNCTAD can be called the second segment. During this period, Dr. Singh got rare experience into the international work culture and learnt at first hand the levers of international economic diplomacy.

Dr. Singh's two-decade long innings while serving the Government of India as an Economic Administrator and Planner is the longest and the third segment. During this period, Dr. Singh came to grips with the unique problems and solutions that are relevant to the Indian context.

And, Dr. Singh's decade-and-a-half-and-still-continuing innings as Finance Minister, Rajya Sabha Member, Leader of Opposition and finally as Prime Minister is the fourth segment. If morning shows the day, this should be the most enduring chapter of Dr. Singh's illustrious career.

If one judges by the longest amount of time spent by Dr. Singh in any one position throughout his career, it has been that of the Finance Minister of the country, not counting his Rajya Sabha innings of 13-year-plus. Both being in the domain of public life, which has catapulted this lad from faceless Gah in far away West Punjab into the position of India's Prime Minister, it seems that Dr. Singh has finally dropped anchor in public life.

From the very beginning, Dr. Singh was academically brilliant and had turned topping in his University a matter of habit.

Early Promise

It was way back in the year 1948, barely a year after India gained independence from British colonial rule, that Manmohan Singh matriculated from the Punjab University with a First Class. The young lad was just about 16 years of age at that time, but already showed promise that a brilliant academic career was in store for him.

Just two years after his matriculation, Manmohan Singh cleared his Intermediate, this time securing the first position in the entire Punjab University. Manmohan then pursued Economics (Honours) from the same Punjab University, and two years later, in 1952, repeated his Intermediate feat by once again topping in the University. For this achievement, he received the University Medal for standing first in BA Economics that year.

Manmohan did not rest on his oars. He took up his Masters in Economics and lo and behold, went on to secure the first position in the University just two years down the road in 1954. For this sterling achievement, Manmohan Singh was awarded Punjab University's Uttar Chand Kapur

Medal for standing first in MA (Economics).

Manmohan Singh then went on to do his Economics Tripos (First Class Honours) from the University of Cambridge in England, which he completed in the year 1957, when just 25 years of age. Meanwhile, in 1955, he was awarded the Adam Smith Prize of this University. At Cambridge in 1954, he also got the Wright's Prize for distinguished performance.

Relying on Hard Work

Who would have thought that this frail lad from dusty Gah would have it in him to reach such heights of academic achievements? But the determination was there in little Mohna's mind as is revealed by a story narrated by his cousin sister. She recalls that when his aunt would ask Mohna to finish his milk and said that he would get good marks by drinking the milk, Mohna would say in a measured tone, "I will come first because of my hard work".

Yes, Manmohan Singh kept on working hard and coming first, adding feather after feather to his cap, till his intellectual worth forced his selection for the top job in India.

In 1957, Manmohan Singh was elected Wrenbury Scholar at the University of Cambridge.

Manmohan Singh then went on to pursue his D. Phil., from the Nuffield College of the University of Oxford. In another indication of what was in store for this brilliant lad, his topic, even in the early sixties, was "India's Export Trends and Prospects for Self-Sustained Growth". He accomplished his D. Phil. in the year 1962, and his effort was published in 1964 by the Clarendon Press, Oxford.

After his Economics Tripos from the University of Cambridge in 1957, Manmohan Singh became a Senior Lecturer in Economics at the Punjab University, Chandigarh, which position he held for two years till 1959, when he became a Reader. Continuing with the Punjab University, Manmohan Singh became a Professor of Economics in 1963, and continued in that capacity till 1965. His teaching stint at the Punjab University thus lasted about eight years, from 1957 to 1965.

Career Shift

A shift occurred in Manmohan Singh's career at this point of time. From a brilliant academic, he also became an Economic Administrator. In 1966, he joined the UNCTAD, United Nations Secretariat, New York, as an Economic Affairs Officer. The same year, he became the Chief, Financing for Trade Section, and worked at this position for three years until 1969.

During his stint with UNCTAD, Dr. Manmohan Singh represented the UNCTAD Secretary-General at several inter-governmental meetings, including the Second Session of UNCTAD in 1968, and in the Committee on Invisibles and Financing Related to Trade. He also discharged his duties as Consultant to UNCTAD, ESCAP and Commonwealth Secretariat.

Dr. Singh then returned to the teaching profession, but this time in India's capital, New Delhi, in the capacity of Professor of International Trade at the Delhi School of

Economics, University of Delhi, from 1969 till 1971. As it turned out, this was Dr. Singh's final stint as a Professor.

What happened next was another turning point in Dr. Manmohan Singh's career, as he joined the Government of India in the capacity of an Economic Administrator, went on to hold top positions in this field, which paved the way for his becoming India's Finance Minister and ultimately the Prime Minister of the country.

Economic Administrator

In 1971, after his stint in the Delhi School of Economics, Dr Manmohan Singh became the Economic Advisor in India's Ministry of Foreign Trade. Within a year he became the Chief Economic Advisor in India's Ministry of Finance, which strategically important position he held from 1972 till 1976.

Dr. Manmohan Singh, in the next four years, from November 1976, till April 1980, became the Member for Finance first in India's Space Commission and then in the Atomic Energy Commission, and then the Secretary, Department of Economic Affairs in the Ministry of Finance.

From April 1980 till September 1982, Dr. Singh served as the Member-Secretary in India's Planning Commission. Then he became the Governor, Reserve Bank of India, till January 14, 1985.

Dr. Singh had been part of the Indian delegation to the Third Session of UNCTAD in Santiago in April-May 1972 and to the meetings of the UNCTAD Trade & Development Board, Geneva, from May 1971 to July 1972.

He was part of the Indian delegation at the annual meetings of the International Monetary Fund, IBRD and the Commonwealth Finance Ministers between 1972 and 1979.

Dr. Manmohan Singh was the Deputy for India on the IMF Committee of Twenty for Monetary Reforms from 1972 to 1974. He was the Associate at the IMF Interim Committee and the Joint Fund-Bank Development Committee from 1976 to 1980 and from 1982 to 1985.

Dr. Singh was the Alternate Governor for India, on the Board of Governors of the IBRD and also of the Asian Development Bank, Manila, from 1976 to 1980.

He was the Alternate Governor for India, on the Board of Governors of the IMF from 1982 till 1985. Dr. Singh was the Governor for India on the Board of Governors of the IMF and the International Bank for Reconstruction and Development from 1991 to 1995.

Meanwhile, Dr. Singh was the leader of the Indian delegation to the meeting of the Indo-Soviet Monitoring Group in 1982, the leader of the Indo-Soviet Joint Planning Group between 1980 and 1982 and the Aid India Consortium meetings between 1977 and 1979.

After the assignment as the RBI Governor, Dr. Singh took charge as the Deputy Chairman of the Planning Commission in January 1985, and served in this capacity till July-end 1987, when he became the Secretary-General and Commissioner of the South Commission to continue in this position till November 1990.

In December the same year, Dr. Singh became the Advisor to the Indian Prime Minister on Economic Affairs for a brief budget-making period of four months up to March 1991, and spent three months thereafter, up to June 20, 1991, as the Chairman of the University Grants Commission.

Hectic Time

The twenty-year period from 1971 to 1991, the two decades between Dr Manmohan Singh's Professorship in the Delhi School of Economics (1971) and his becoming India's Finance Minister (1991), were very hectic for Dr. Singh, when he flitted from one assignment to the other, moving with restless energy to give his very best in the service of the nation in the capacity of a leader who leads from the front.

It is the wealth of varied experience that Dr. Singh gained in these two decades that gave him a clear vision of how to bring about economic progress by empowering the people to leverage their latent talents.

Turning Point

The year 1991 brought yet another turning point in his illustrious career. Very busy years in academics and administration had been brought by previous turning points, and now the winds of change brought public life into his lap. The then Prime Minister, Mr. P V Narasimha Rao, chose him to be his Finance Minister, which office Dr. Singh assumed on June 21, 1991.

It is noteworthy that Dr. Singh was not a member of India's Parliament when he was chosen as the Finance

Minister. He became the Finance Minister purely on the strength of his intellectual brilliance and financial expertise. Finance Minister Manmohan Singh became a member of Rajya Sabha, the Upper House of India's Parliament, only in September 1991.

Dr. Singh served as the Finance Minister in Mr. Narasimha Rao's cabinet for the full term of the government until May 15, 1996, serving as India's Finance Minister for five years. Incidentally, this was the longest span of time that Dr. Singh served on one post throughout his career, either in academics or as an economic administrator.

Dropping Anchor

Indicating that Dr. Manmohan Singh had finally dropped anchor, this brilliant academic and noted administrator got re-elected to Rajya Sabha for six-year terms first in June 1995 and then in June 2001.

Meanwhile, in December 2000, a great feather was put in Dr. Singh's cap. The United Nations Secretary General appointed him as a Member of a Group of Eminent Persons to advise him on Financing for Development.

From March 1998, till he became Prime Minister on May 22, 2004, Dr. Manmohan Singh was the Leader of Opposition in Rajya Sabha.

In 1987, Dr. Singh was honoured with the Padma Vibhushan Award by the President of India.

He became an Honorary Professor of the Delhi School of Economics in 1996.

In the year 1994, Dr. Singh was elected a Distinguished Fellow of the London School of Economics, Centre for Asia, Economy, Politics and Society. In the same year, he was elected the Honorary Fellow of the Nuffield College, University of Oxford, United Kingdom.

In 1982, he was elected the Honorary Fellow of the St. John's College, Cambridge, United Kingdom, and in 1976 the Honorary Fellow of the Jawaharlal Nehru University, New Delhi.

Leading the Team

Given his half-a-century of contributions to economic development, as an intellectual and an administrator, it is little wonder that the post of prime minister sits lightly on the shoulder of Dr. Manmohan Singh. Dr. Singh leads the team that the Indian council of ministers is, and the larger team that the entire country is, on the strength of his intellectual prowess, his experience and his achievements. It is only natural, then, that Dr. Manmohan Singh enjoys support, and respect, cutting across party lines, and the lines of region, caste and community.

Any selfish Indian may be excused for hoping that Dr. Singh has dropped anchor in Indian politics and destiny would not one day take him to the field of international diplomacy, to spearhead the global effort against poverty, want, hunger and misery.

But then, his career graph shows that Dr. Manmohan Singh is a true Karmayogi, standing first in the University, or in life, by the sheer dint of his hard work. A Karmayogi does not look at the rewards of his labour, but his work is reward in itself.

Dr. Manmohan Singh, as the Prime Minister of a coalition government, wears a crown of thorns. However, Dr. Singh is an achiever who has the capacity to deliver results even in the most difficult of situations.

Manmohan Singh & Sonia Gandhi - Team Work to Develop India

Sonia Gandhi - The Soul is Indian

Prime Minister's offerings to
'Bapu' Father of the Nation
at Raj Ghat, New Delhi

PM Dr. Manmohan Singh,
along with Congress President Sonia Gandhi for a
prayer meeting on Jawaharlal Nehru's death anniversary

CHAPTER

5

It is Sonia-Manmohan Combine

When the Indian Prime Minister, Dr. Manmohan Singh, took the oath of office and secrecy as India's 13th Prime Minister on May 22, 2004, he became the first Sikh Prime Minister of India.

To mark this landmark oath taking, Gurudwaras (Sikh places of worship) were lit up in all their grandeur in New Delhi and in other cities. Even in far away Assam, the state Dr. Manmohan Singh represents in the Rajya Sabha, there was much dancing and celebration. At the Rajib Bhawan, where the Assam State Congress Party's Headquarters is located, huge cutouts of Dr. Manmohan Singh and

Mrs. Sonia Gandhi were put up atop the building. Also, a huge screen was put up at the Rajib Bhawan to show the live telecast of the oath-taking ceremony of Dr. Manmohan Singh and his 68-member Council of Ministers.

And, when India's President, Dr. A P J Abdul Kalam, administered the oath of office to Dr. Manmohan Singh, it was the first time in the history of the Indian Republic that a President from a minority community was swearing in a Prime Minister who hailed from another minority community.

Apolitical Personalities

Dr. Kalam, is a renowned scientist and is known as the moving force behind India's nuclear programme. And, Dr. Manmohan Singh is a world-renowned economist who has made his mark in the Universities of Oxford and Cambridge. Dr. Singh is known as the architect of India's economic reforms that have succeeded in delivering unprecedented economic growth to the country and quite some strength to the economy. Both Kalam and Singh are known to be largely apolitical personalities. They are recognized as professionals and achievers who are above politics.

Non-politicians like Dr. Kalam and Dr. Singh adorning the two top posts in India is something entirely new for this country. This marks a clear departure from the past when lifelong politicians ran the country as Prime Ministers and Presidents. The President's post was invariably a reward for a loyal political career. In the year 2004, a top scientist and a top economist have been charged with running the affairs of the country, large numbers of whose citizens are not happy with the conduct of the politicians as a class.

The twin-team of Kalam and Singh has the potential to inspire the nation and to bring about a refreshing change in the way that public affairs are conducted. They can galvanize the Great Indian Middle Class out of its apathy and turn it into a proactive participant in nation building.

The Kalam-Singh combination may be co-incidental but is quite significant as it reflects the desire of the Indian people who would like to see clean, upright, knowledgeable professionals, who are achievers, being at the helm of the country's affairs.

Politics can not be Wished Away

However, despite the fact that both Dr. Kalam and Dr. Singh are not the typical Indian politician, 'politics' cannot be wished away from the Manmohan Singh coalition. It was only an indication of the things to come when the various constituents of the Manmohan Singh government were engaged in a most embarrassing tug-of-war for berths in the council of ministers during the run-up to the swearing-in.

The man of action that Dr. Manmohan Singh is, he got straight down to business soon after he took oath, immediately taking charge of his office.

Prime Minister Manmohan Singh has thus got a golden opportunity to make the 21st century the century of India. The Sonia-Manmohan combine is ideally equipped to move in that direction. But the time is short, for, come 2006, electoral politics will once again overshadow everything else on India's political radar, as a clutch of state assembly elections come on the horizon.

Youth, the Deciding Factor

It is now realized that the young Indian voter was the deciding factor in Elections 2004. The mascots of the BJP were in their late 70s and also physically weak and uninspiring and often displaying symptoms of failing memory. This stood in sharp contrast to the agility, charm, vivacity and the spirit of life possessed by their prime challenger, Mrs. Sonia Gandhi. The youthful candidates so thoughtfully fielded by the Congress Party, including Jyotiraditya Sindhia, Sandeep Dixit, Sachin Pilot and Govinda identified with today's India that wishes to confidently stride on the world stage. Yes, the Congress Party was able to get the youth on its side in a large measure.

Without doubt the dimpled good looks, the clean-cut charm, the apparent simplicity despite his very eminent background, and the confidence of youth that Rahul Gandhi possesses, did play a decisive role in swaying the younger voters towards the Congress Party. And, the Indira Gandhi-like magnetism that her granddaughter, Priyanka Gandhi, commands remained the final weapon in the Congress Party's armoury that was never fully utilized.

If the Rahul-Priyanka duo had put their shoulders to the oars a couple of weeks earlier than they did in the 2004 elections, perhaps the Congress Party would have managed a majority on its own, rather than being dependent on the aged patriarchs of Left parties like Comrade Harkishan Singh Surjeet and Comrade Jyoti Basu.

It is quite possible that had Rahul and Priyanka campaigned in a much bigger way in Elections 2004, many doddering politicians belonging to a by-gone era of Indian politics would have been forced to go into retirement.

Yes, Dr. Manmohan Singh was 72 years of age when he took office of Prime Minister. But he is a very active person, full of energy and with a razor-sharp mind. Moreover, he has the advantage of the Youth Brigade being in the Congress Party. It is now for Mrs Sonia Gandhi and Dr. Manmohan Singh to channel the energies of the youth that have gravitated towards the Congress Party.

Disconcerting

It is, however, somewhat disconcerting to see in the Manmohan Singh council of ministers such individuals who are so impacted by age that they can't emerge from a car without assistance. It is again a dampener when politicians from half-a-century ago are over-eager to address press conferences and put a spanner in the works.

Media reports claimed that the Bihar strongman, Mr. Laloo Prasad Yadav, had demanded the Home Ministry for himself. This demand was apparently not acceded to by the Congress Party, which dominates the coalition. After all, Laloo Yadav has court cases against him, filed by the CBI, involving serious charges of corruption and misappropriation of funds as also possessing assets disproportionate to known sources of income. How could such a person be made the Indian Home Minister? After all, Lalooji had resigned as the Bihar Chief Minister when the cases came to court, and his wife, Mrs. Rabri Devi, was installed as the State's Chief Minister.

On being rebuffed, a smarting Mr. Laloo Prasad Yadav was supposed to have gone into hiding, inaccessible even to the media. After a while, he surfaced to say that what he was seeking was an economic package for Bihar to offset the loss that the state had suffered due to years of neglect by the Center, and by the partition of the state when Jharkhand was carved out of Bihar, leaving a rump that has less resources.

Laloo's Clout

However, Laloo was able to wrest as many as eight berths in the Union council of ministers for his Rashtriya Janata Dal, the highest number after the Congress Party's 42 and one more than the DMK's 7.

Mr. Ram Vilas Paswan of the Lok Janshakti Party, a pre-poll ally of the Congress Party, reportedly sulked till the last moment over not getting the post of the Cabinet Minister for Railways. It was not clear if Paswan was more peeved over not getting this post of his choice or over talk that this post would go to his apparent rival in Bihar politics, Mr. Laloo Prasad Yadav. Paswan is said to have spent hours at the 10 Janpath residence of Mrs. Sonia Gandhi to negotiate the best deal though in public he denied this being the purpose of his extended parleys with Soniaji on the morning of the swearing-in ceremony.

In the end, it was the former Prime Minister, Mr. Vishwanath Pratap Singh, who played a significant role in creating this anti-BJP, Congress-led alliance, who persuaded the sulking Paswan to come to the swearing-in ceremony at the grand Ashoka Hall of the Rashtrapati Bhawan. It so happened that Paswan and V P Singh landed up at the ceremony just in time in the same car.

At one point of time, the formula worked out to settle the strife was one berth in the Union Cabinet for every four seats held in Parliament by a coalition partner. This was later improved to one berth for 3.5 seats. Considering that the formation of the Manmohan Singh government began with so much haggling and bad blood, one can imagine the amount of time and energy the new Prime Minister would have to devote to keeping the mutually-warring coalition partners on board and in good humour.

Wry Smile

Reflecting this sad state of affairs is an incident that occurred as the swearing-in was in progress. Comrade Sitaram Yechuri of the CPI (M) sent a note to Prime Minister Singh, which essentially said that many of those being sworn in would be happy over the fact that the Left Parties did not join the government and supported it from outside, thus leaving the ministerial berths for others. Dr. Singh is reported to have smiled wryly on reading the note.

The Paswan and Laloo Yadav episodes are cited as just two instances of the pulls and pressures at work in the Manmohan Singh-led coalition government, and there are quite a few other instances, including those of lobbying/warring within the Congress Party for plum posts.

It remains to be seen how Dr. Manmohan Singh, who seems to have been pressured into accepting this situation without cracking the whip, will involve the Laloo-brigade, which is a significant grouping in the Union Council of ministers, in the task of framing and implementing national policies and programmes.

A preview of the continuing pulls and pressures that will operate on Dr. Manmohan Singh was evident at the very first sitting of the council of ministers with the Prime Minister in the chair. For the first time ever, a meeting of the Cabinet was held without the assigning of portfolios to the members. This could not be done obviously because the interminable negotiations were on, and issues remained to be sorted out among the warring partners.

Begin with a Compromise

Also, since the composition of the council of ministers was clearly not out of the choice of Dr. Manmohan Singh, but was the product of sheer political blackmail and brinkmanship by so-called allies demanding a bigger slice of the cake for their chosen few, quite a few criminally charge-sheeted individuals found their way into Dr. Manmohan Singh's council of ministers.

The main opposition Bharatya Janata Party, which had been deflated after Mrs. Sonia Gandhi made the "sacrifice" of the Prime Minister's post when it was hers for the taking, found a God-sent issue in this. Pointed out Mr. Arun Jaitley, a prominent lawyer and a spokesman for the BJP, that half-a-dozen members of the Dr. Manmohan Singh council of ministers were facing charges in court in such cases as corruption, possessing assets disproportionate to known sources of income, extortion and mafia activities.

Such a composition of the council of ministers headed by a sparkling clean Prime Minister like Dr Manmohan Singh is indeed ironical, and can only be explained by compulsions of coalition politics.

However, if Dr Manmohan Singh continues to succumb to such political compulsions and keeps on doing the bidding of his unreasonable allies, the day may come sooner rather than later when he would lose the body-armour of a person who is above politics and is sparkling clean. After all, a person is known by the company he keeps.

As Finance Minister, Dr Manmohan Singh could remain clean and above politics even as he rubbed shoulders in the Narasimha Rao cabinet with half-a-dozen unadulterated politicians who were later charge-sheeted by courts.

Perception as Important as Fact

However, Dr. Singh's image, as the leader of the present cabinet, would not remain clean and apolitical if there is a perception that he has inducted into the council of ministers those who are involved in dirty politics or are charge-sheeted for criminal activity.

On the other hand, if the public perceives that it is not Dr. Singh who chose this council of ministers but his coalition partners did that deed, some of the mud thrown at him on this score would not stick.

That brings us to another aspect for the Dr. Manmohan Singh government, which may assume serious proportions as his Prime Ministership endures. Who is actually running the government? Is it Dr. Singh? Or, is it Mrs. Sonia Gandhi who is pulling the strings?

Without doubt, Dr. Manmohan Singh did not become Prime Minister of India as a matter of right. He had never even dreamt of becoming Prime Minister. He went on record to say that he did not expect to be Prime Minister.

Dr. Singh got this coveted post only because Mrs. Sonia Gandhi, who for reasons best known to her, declined to accept the position, and nominated him as Prime Minister.

The entire Congress Party, which had been beseeching and imploring Mrs. Sonia Gandhi till the very last moment to change her mind, finally fell in line and accepted Dr. Singh as Prime Minister only because she wished it so. After taking oath of office, the first thing that Dr. Manmohan Singh did was to walk across the Ashok Hall in full public view to where Mrs. Sonia Gandhi was sitting to pay his respects.

Sonia-Manmohan Team

Not just Dr. Singh but most other Congress Party's oath-taking members went ahead and offered their regards to Mrs. Sonia Gandhi after joining the council of ministers.

Even during the interminable delay constituting the run-up to the oath-taking, Mrs. Gandhi, operating from her 10, Janpath residence, played a central role in deciding the composition of the Union Cabinet, and the aspiring allies made a beeline to her.

The point is that even as Dr. Manmohan Singh formally began his term as Prime Minister, the real Prime Minister calling the shots from a separate centre of power remained Mrs. Sonia Gandhi. Analysts have drawn a parallel in this with the Shiv Sena, run by Mr. Bala Saheb Thackeray in Mumbai. Thackeray is described as the "remote control" that runs the Shiv Sena through the various functionaries he nominates whenever Shiv Sena comes to power. Thackeray runs the party with an iron hand and is the final arbiter in all matters.

It is speculated that Mrs. Sonia Gandhi may well be a very active remote control taking all the important decisions from her 10, Janpath residence, while Dr Manmohan Singh remains the formal face of the government.

Ideal Division of Labour

If that is the case, the resultant situation may well suit an intellectual of Dr. Manmohan Singh's calibre, for, it represents an efficient division of labour. Mrs. Sonia Gandhi's ability to attract votes for the Congress Party and the fact that she has inherited the Nehru-Gandhi family's legacy, gives her the clout to speak the final word in all political matters that may come up before the newly-formed, broad anti-BJP alliance. This would take a burden off Dr. Manmohan Singh's shoulders, relieving him of a political responsibility that he may not relish, or he may not be well equipped to carry out.

This arrangement would leave Dr. Singh free to take care of that which he knows best, i.e. minding and mending India's economy, not as Finance Minister, but as Prime Minister of the country. Soon after assuming office, Dr. Singh set before himself a target of achieving an 8 per cent growth rate for the economy that would also generate employment, ending the stagnation of agriculture, reviving manufacturing and empowering the Indian people to leverage their latent talents. That, in a nutshell, may well be Dr. Manmohan Singh's overall mantra for the Indian economy.

It may be noted that Dr. Singh is found shy in commenting on issues that are remotely political, except to repeat what the Congress Party's election manifesto promised. Even the Common Minimum Programme according to which the Manmohan Singh-government would function, was crafted largely at the residence of Mrs. Sonia Gandhi, where the leaders of coalition partners were invited to discuss the nitty-gritty.

A Good Arrangement

This apparent division of labour between Mrs. Sonia Gandhi and Dr. Manmohan Singh on the lines of political and economic matters, which may be called the Sonia-Manmohan-combine for want of a formal name, may in fact be a good thing and also eminently efficient. There would be nothing to be diffident about in such an arrangement, which can get to grips with the business of running the country on the bedrock of a secular polity and society while at the same time achieving rapid economic growth that can make the 21st century a century of India, as the former Prime Minister late Rajiv Gandhi, had visualized.

For the success of the Sonia-Manmohan combine, which sits at the helm of the newly forged anti-BJP alliance, it needs to deliver some quick results and a new programme of action that can fire the imagination of the nation, especially the youth. If Dr. Manmohan Singh and Mrs. Sonia Gandhi can deliver some positives to the youth in a substantial manner and in the near-to-medium term of within two years, that would make it very difficult for the BJP and its NDA allies to claw their way back to the center-stage of Indian politics from the abyss of the stunning electoral defeat that they find themselves in.

Dr. Manmohan Singh made it clear that the defence of the secular fabric of the country will be among his top priorities. He has also promised to create an environment that facilitates the realization of the latent talents of the countrymen. The Prime Minister has talked of ushering in a development strategy that will be "inclusive" and will empower the people. He has dedicated himself to achieving an eight percent growth rate for the economy that will not be "jobless".

Making a Difference

All of the above indicate how the Manmohan Singh government's policies and programmes would be different from the ones implemented by the previous Atal Behari Vajpayee government of the National Democratic Alliance. Defence of secularism, creating economic opportunities for the countrymen, creating growth along with jobs and reaching the benefits of reforms to the poor and the deprived would be areas where it is perceived that the previous government may have been lax and the Manmohan Singh government would pull up its socks..

The Ex Union Minister for Finance Dr. Manmohan Singh giving TV interview after presenting the Union Budget for the year 1991-92 to the parliament

Dr. Manmohan Singh : '*A Czar of Economic Reforms*'

The Mauritius Ex PM, Mr. Anerood Jugannath greeting the Ex Union Minister for Finance Dr. Manmohan Singh at the dinner hosted in the former's honour, by Ex PM P.V. Narasimha Rao

The Ex PM P.V. Narasimha Rao, leaving for Jakarta to attend the 10th Non-Aligned Summit greeted by Dr. Singh and others

The Ex Union Minister for Finance Dr. Manmohan Singh in a meeting with the representatives of Trade Unions in New Delhi

The Ex Governor, R.B.I., Dr. Manmohan Singh called on
H.E. Dr. Jurgen Warnke, Minister of FRG,
in New Delhi on Sept. 17, 1982

CHAPTER

6

What Makes Manmohan Singh Tick?

What makes Dr. Manmohan Singh tick? What is there in this extraordinary person that has brought him to the most powerful post in the country? What lies behind his nation-wide popularity that cuts across party lines, as also the divides of caste, community and region?

Doing His Duty

Dr. Singh is a firm believer in, and often quotes, the dictum contained in the *Bhagavad Gita*, according to which an individual should continue to do his duty and not bother about the rewards. Dr. Singh's life is a story of hard work without bothering about the fruits of that hard work.

Dr. Singh says that to do one's duty without expectation of results is the guiding principle of not just the *Bhagavad Gita* but also of all scriptures, including the *Guru Granth Sahib*.

Dr. Singh is a religious man, visits the gurudwara, and has an abiding faith in God.

His Heart Beats for India

Dr. Singh is also very proud of the Indian civilization. He is proud to be an Indian and is patriotic to the core. He is fond of quoting the famous couplet penned by Allama Iqbal, which runs thus, "*Iran-o-Misr-o-Roma, Sab Mit Gaye Jahan Se, Koi Baat Hai Ki Hastee Mit tee nahin hamari. ... Sadiyon Raha hai dushman daure jahan hamara.*" [Great civilizations like Iran, Egypt and Rome have all vanished. There must be a reason that our civilization endures, (even though) the world has been our foe for centuries.]

Dr. Singh says that while some people in India may have forgotten God, India has not been forgotten by God. The 5000-year-old Indian civilization is still vibrant and our civilization has stood the test of time.

Dr. Singh, whose intellectual brilliance has been recognized the world over, has, through his distinguished career, had many offers from abroad, but refused them only because he wants to work for India. It is his patriotism that has inspired Dr. Singh to do his best for the betterment of the lot of his countrymen.

Dr. Singh wants to give back to society as much as he can, for, he does not forget that a great amount of his own education has been funded by scholarships.

Man of his Principles

Dr. Singh is a man of his principles, and will not compromise them on any account, say those who have known him well. He will not compromise on his core values even if he has to suffer personal loss, they say.

Honest to the core, Dr. Singh does not ever use his official transport for personal use. In his years in various positions with the government of India, Dr. Singh has used government resources only for the purpose for which they were meant. Even if his closest relatives drop in, he would prefer to pay their taxi bill, rather than have them dropped by the government transport at his disposal. Even during his official assignments abroad, Dr. Singh is known to have spent his allowance money specifically on the purpose for which it was meant. This level of honesty and uprightness is extremely rare for a government servant in India, and endears Dr. Singh to the Indian masses, that are sick and tired of government functionaries who are corrupt to the core.

Despite his towering status, Dr. Singh is an extremely humble man. There are no airs about him and no bloated ego. The false sense of self-importance that marks the persona of most Indian politicians is conspicuous by its absence in Dr. Singh. A student or a professional, in fact any average Indian, can approach him and Dr. Singh shows no impatience or irritation. Rather, his warmth and the personal interest that he takes in all those he meets, leave a lasting impression. Of course, as a Prime Minister, Dr. Manmohan Singh's approachability is markedly curtailed, but that is the demand of his high office, not his personal preference.

Dr. Singh considers the taxpayer's money to be sacred and wishes that every ten rupees should go the farthest in getting benefits to the Indian people. He is known to prefer to travel economy class even when he was entitled to something higher.

Dr. Singh is fond of reading books on history, politics and economics, especially biographies of great men and women. It is said that it was his interest in reading that changed the very course of his life. It so happened that Manmohan Singh's father wanted him to study medicine. The young lad even enrolled to study to be a doctor. But then he read Minoo Masani's book, *Our India* and his passion for economics was aroused. The result was a change of stream for Manmohan Singh, say those close to him.

Fond of Music

Dr. Singh has a weakness for classical Indian music and M S Subbalakshmi is among his favourites.

It seems that Dr. Singh is a combination of two persons at the same time. He is simple, humble, decent and gentle and comes across as the next door neighbour at first sight. However, interacting with him, even by way of listening to his lecture in a class, or his presentation at a seminar, and one is struck by Manmohan Singh's unique vision, his stunningly effective ideas, his undaunted will and his great energy. Yes, both these sets of virtues are in the same individual who has become India's Prime Minister, thus also acquiring the power, and opportunity, to translate his vision and his ideas into reality.

Dr. Singh considers it of paramount importance to revive the confidence of Indians in themselves, in the country and in the government.

Good at Reconciling Differences

Dr. Singh is a non-controversial figure. He is neither aggressive nor offensive. It is with the truth in his argument that he is patiently able to convince the other side to change their views. Dr. Singh has the foresight and the knack to see any situation in its correct perspective and bring about improvements through timely correctives. It is this ability that enables Dr Singh to reconcile differing approaches and fashion them into a single policy instrument. Of course, this unique strength possessed by Dr. Singh will be put to the test during his tenure as Prime Minister when he reconciles the approach of the Left and of the Congress Party to deliver the promised results to the voters.

The fact that Dr. Singh is unlike the typical Indian politician, his brilliance and his uprightness, his commitment to the national interest and his personal honesty, his ability to lead and his capacity to come up with solutions that work, have all combined to create quite some excitement in the country and among Indians outside the country in the immediate aftermath of Dr. Singh becoming Prime Minister.

This excitement is in part a salute to the unique strength of the Indian democracy that enables a non-seeker like Dr. Singh to be Prime Minister. The excitement is also a sign of hope, that at long last the country may be rid of politics that is unseemly, to say the least. It is the conviction of the average Indian that Dr. Manmohan Singh can never be a wheeler-dealer, and would never bank on political-fixers.

Many of even those who admired the outgoing Prime Minister, Mr. Atal Behari Vajpayee, find in Dr Singh the right person to have succeeded Vajpayee. It is believed by many that Singh will carry forward the good work that the Vajpayee government was doing, even as he modifies the policies and programmes to better suit the country.

Cross Country Acceptability

It is a sign of Dr. Singh's cross-country acceptability as Prime Minister, that the major opposition Bharatiya Janata Party has apparently taken a decision not to train its guns at the Prime Minister. Instead, the object of BJP's criticism would be the Congress President, Mrs. Sonia Gandhi, it has been reported. This apparent tactical decision by the BJP seems to be motivated either by respect for Dr. Singh or out of realization that no mud thrown at Dr. Singh would stick, or both.

Thus, with Dr. Singh becoming the Prime Minister of the country, there is an air of expectancy and of optimism. Dr. Singh has the ability to be equal to this expectancy. Optimism is itself a resource that can be positively harnessed.

Those who have come in contact with Dr. Singh during his long career have largely been impressed by his ideas and his approach. It is to be seen if Dr. Singh can similarly fire the imaginations of the political beings that constitute the support for his government. If Dr. Singh can have an educating influence on the unadulterated politicians with whom he would be rubbing shoulders in his council of ministers and in the consultative committee to implement the common minimum programme, he would have done a great service to the nation. And, if he can bring them around to his point of view as far as taking the economy forward is considered, it would iron out the wrinkles in his coalition so essential for effective functioning.

A Potential Mass Leader

It seems that while Dr. Singh is not a mass leader, he has great convincing ability and leadership attributes when having one-to-one interactions or when addressing smaller gatherings. The latter form of interaction has enabled Dr. Singh to influence a large number of people over the decades. These people constitute a solid support base for Dr. Singh, but are not concentrated in one constituency but are spread all over the country and abroad.

Satellite television has the ability to magnify the impact of one-to-one interaction by giving it a national scale. When Dr. Singh appears on television at midday after the worst-ever morning crash in the Indian stock markets, he is able to influence a sufficient number of investors to ensure an immediate rebound of the market. And, when the television news channels show him making the statement that he believes in the patriotism of his coalition partners, he is not only addressing those partners but a wider national audience that is equally patriotic.

The point is that Dr. Singh can emerge as a mass leader with great countrywide following and respect, even as he is not strictly a political being. It is his sincerity and his embodiment of the ethos of this country in his personal conduct that gives him a persona that is larger than any office and gives him a head start on any politician.

Yes, the fact that Dr. Manmohan Singh is an average Indian at heart, and not the typical politician, is what makes him tick, and catapults him to higher and higher offices without him actually craving for them.

Economic Vision document being released in 2004

Mani Shankar Aiyar and other Congress Leaders greeting Mr. Singh in 1993

An election year budget, 1995

Dr. Manmohan Singh with Ex PM P.V. Narasimha Rao, who is presiding over a full meeting of the Planning Commission

Ex PM P.V. Narasimha Rao addressing the 44th meeting of the National Development Council, the Ex Union Minister for Finance Dr. Manmohan Singh and the Ex Deputy Chairman, Planning Commission, Pranab Mukherjee are also present

The Ex Union Minister for Finance Dr. Manmohan Singh
in conversation with the Chairman of Asian Development Bank
who called on him

The Ex Union Minister for Finance Dr. Manmohan Singh
in conversation with the Vice President of the
Commission of the European Community,
H.E. Mr. Frad Andruessen who called on him

P. Chidambaram - Determination to Boost the Economy

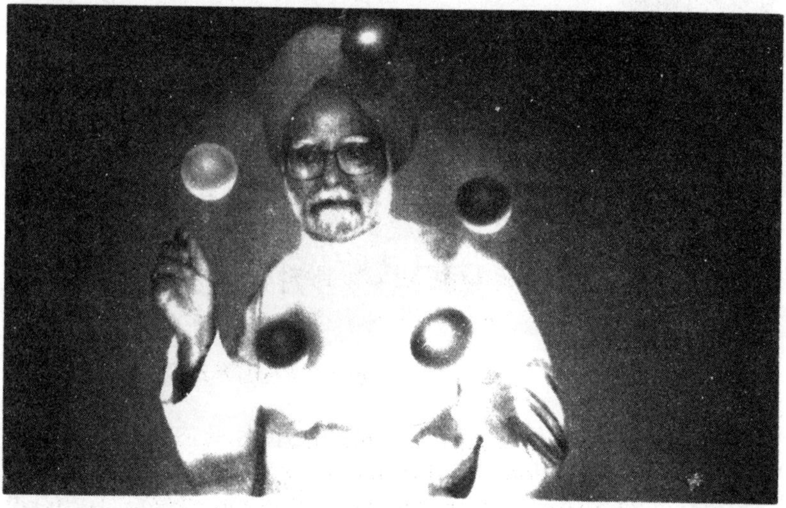

Prime Minister with Magical Wand

CHAPTER

7

Economist with the Magic Wand

Dr. Manmohan Singh's five years as India's Finance Minister under Prime Minister P V Narasimha Rao from 1991 to 1996 not only changed the face of the Indian economy, but also transformed the way the Indian government ran the economy.

Crisis Situation

It was a crisis situation in 1991 when Prime Minister Rao picked Dr. Singh to be the Finance Minister. When Dr. Singh heard the news, he was astonished. He had never imagined that he would be made Finance Minister. Some of his friends and colleagues told him that this might not be a genuine offer, since the dire straits of the Indian economy could not be improved in a hurry. They felt that a scapegoat would be made out of Dr. Singh and his tenure as Finance Minister may not last long. They advised that he should not take up the offer. How wrong they were!

Accepting the Slender Chance

Dr. Singh knew that the Indian economy was in a complete mess. Yet, he believed that there did exist a slender chance of reviving the economy with some hard work and some policy changes in a matter of three years. He decided to take the chance.

Thus began Dr. Singh's innings in politics, which, apparently he has come to relish, having spent some thirteen years in the Rajya Sabha.

While initially briefing Prime Minister Rao on the state of the economy, it was made clear by Singh that India had foreign exchange reserves of just about US dollars one billion, sufficient only to pay for a week's imports for the country. Deficit financing was so high a percentage of the GDP that it could not be sustained. In any case, lenders were no longer willing to finance the deficit. And, there was real danger of the country defaulting on its foreign loan repayments.

Singh sought a free hand from the Prime Minister to address the fundamental problems of the Indian economy so as to create an environment for businesses to grow and the inherent entrepreneurial skills of the countrymen to be leveraged. To the credit of Prime Minister Rao, Singh got this free hand.

Dr. Singh was very forthright in saying that he wanted the "government off the back of the Indian people", to leave them alone to do work and provide strength to the economy.

As Singh went ahead to release the Indian economy from the vice-like grip of a corruption and delay-generating bureaucracy, there were protests not only from those whose powers were being curbed but also from Members of Parliament, even from Rao's own ruling party, who did not see eye-to-eye with what Manmohan Singh was doing.

Silencing the Critics

The ingenious way out around this opposition that Dr. Singh found at that time indicates that he is no greenhorn at politics, as many perceive him to be. Singh referred to the vision of the Late Rajiv Gandhi regarding the unshackling of the talents of the Indian private sector. When Dr. Singh argued that he was only trying to implement the vision of Rajivji, his critics were silenced for the moment.

The permanent silencing of the critics occurred when the Indian economy rebounded within a year or two, after Dr. Singh proceeded to end the economically inefficient license-quota-permit raj. This was even better than Dr. Singh had expected, thus buttressing his faith in the inherent strength of the Indian economy.

While taking the decision to take up the offer to be India's Finance Minister at a most difficult point of time, Singh had thought that he would acquire a "footnote in Indian history" in case he succeeded in reviving the economy. Not only did Singh get that footnote, but his remarkable work as the Finance Minister for five years provided him the foothold in Indian politics which ultimately catapulted him to the office of the country's Prime Minister. He was called the Miracle Man who turned the Indian economy around.

Being a patriotic Indian, Dr. Singh took up the challenge that Rao offered him not just because there was a chance of success but primarily because of his reasoning, "Who fails if India succeeds?" Clearly even in taking that momentous decision, the guiding principle was that he must do his best in the national interest.

Unconventional Prescription

Singh's prescription for the Indian economy at that time was not what was the viewpoint of most of his contemporaries from Oxford and Cambridge. The conventional wisdom at that time was that there has to be a strong government for an economy to be revived and such a government has to be a leading player in the economy. Such a government has not only to create infrastructure, it also has to intervene in the economy to spearhead its growth.

But Dr. Singh delivered great success out of reducing the role of the government in the Indian economy, as a regulator and as a primary player in sectors in which the government should not have been in the first place.

This does not mean that Dr. Singh did not advocate Central Planning. He has voiced his opinion that to achieve rapid growth over a small time frame of, say, two decades, one needs not just Central Planning but also government enterprises, especially when there is shortage of entrepreneurs willing to take risk.

After a period of time, however, such government enterprises generally do not modernize and can even become a drag on the economy, leading to the impression that Central Planning is getting bogged down.

Mixed Economy

After assuming the office of the Prime Minister of the country, Dr. Singh has been emphatic that India needs a strong public sector, and she also needs a strong and vibrant private sector. This is precisely the view that Dr. Singh espoused when he was the Finance Minister. This idea of a mixed economy for India was held by India's first Prime Minister, Pandit Jawaharlal Nehru who was influenced by the British idea of the coexistence of the public and the private sectors.

Dr. Singh feels that the mixed economy concept was Pandit Nehru's modification to the Soviet style of Central Planning.

Dr. Singh agrees that there must be some form of control and rationing when demand far exceeds supply. However, he is of the conviction that the license-quota-permit-raj creates too many delay-generating regulations that in turn create opportunities for corruption, leading to a dampening effect on enterprise.

Dr. Singh acknowledges the progress made by certain economies of East and South East Asia in the seventies and the eighties, South Korea being a shining example, thereby achieving the status of a developed economy in just one generation. In the same period, the Central Planning in India did not deliver economic growth anywhere near the growth rate achieved by these economies!

It remains the objective of Dr. Manmohan Singh to make India a major global economic power. Dr. Manmohan Singh can easily silence any critics in the Congress Party when he goes ahead with implementing the vision of the late Rajiv Gandhi of making the 21st century a century of India.

Contending with the Communists

However, silencing criticism from the Communist Parties, even as he goes ahead with implementing economic reforms, would be a different cup of tea. Dr. Singh is ingenious enough to find middle ground that keeps the Communists on board — after all the government cannot survive a minute without their support — even as he goes ahead with reforming the economy.

Dr. Singh is a firm believer in the unshackling of the Indian economy from too much governance. After assuming office of Prime Minister, Dr. Singh has promised to create an environment in which the latent talents of the Indian people can be leveraged. This may be taken as a pointer to further reducing the stifling governmental role in the economic life of the people of the country.

Dr. Singh also believes that the government has no business being in sectors that are not essential for it to be in. On the other hand, there are sectors like health, social safety and education in which the government must play an enlarged role.

This being the Prime Minister's bent of mind, it is possible that the new government's tenure will see a reorientation of the moneys spent by the government, a greater proportion going into creating infrastructure, thus bringing the changes required with the least amount of disturbance and dislocation.

If Prime Minister Singh attempts to close down, or sell, government enterprises, he is sure to meet strong resistance from his coalition partners. However, there would be no such resistance if Dr. Singh assigns a larger role to the government in such fields as health and education.

There should also be little opposition from coalition partners if the government of Dr. Singh leaves the private sector free to leverage its innovative capabilities to attain prosperity.

Facilitating Prosperity

Clearly, then, even as Dr. Singh may not have the "free hand" that he had when Prime Minister Rao hand-picked him to be the Finance Minister in 1991, he will have sufficient power in his hands in his Prime Ministerial term starting 2004 to be a facilitator for prosperity.

Dr. Singh got only five years as the country's Finance Minister. Many feel that the economy would have been even stronger had Dr. Singh got another five years as Finance Minister, giving him a decade in a row. However, Finance Ministers that succeeded him have primarily carried forward the process that he had initiated. So, many of the policies and programmes initiated by the Vajpayee government including the massive Golden Quadrilateral Scheme, would be continued by Dr. Manmohan Singh.

One area in which Finance Ministers who followed Dr. Manmohan Singh may not have carried forward his prescriptions for the Indian economy is in "getting the government off the back of the Indian people".

Ask the common man and he will tell you that babudom always has him by the scruff of his neck and he can breathe easy only by greasing palms.

Getting the Corrupt off People's Back

Corruption in bureaucracy, and in the police, is so pervasive that it is no longer an issue. Even the country's judiciary has been repeatedly exposed on this count. What use is the removal of the hated license-quota-permit raj if it is only to be replaced by the raj of the corrupt? Things have come to such a pass that doing legitimate business is not remunerative and even otherwise honest businessmen are forced to have illegitimate operations in view of the lower cost of illegitimate operations and for surviving in the market.

For making the 21st century really the century of India, it would be a precondition to get the corrupt off the back of the Indian people, groaning under the unbearable load.

Extortionist-corruption has now taken the shape of a nationwide organized crime, and is no longer a mere social ill. It has become a huge drag on the Indian economy, much like the license-permit-quota raj once was.

Dr. Manmohan Singh has once waived the magic wand in the early 1990s to lift the Indian economy from an abyss. It is to be seen what prescription the good doctor has for the more challenging task of making the 21st century a century of India.

The appointment of learned economist Dr. Sanjay Baru as his media adviser, shows his determination for balancing the good relations among government, media and industries.

Mr. George Bush
President - USA

Mr. Parvez Musharraf
President - Pakistan

CHAPTER

8

Kashmir, Pakistan and the USA

The Indian Prime Minister, Dr. Manmohan Singh, is a picture of dignified simplicity in his trademark loose fitting long *kurta* and *pyjama,* and the neatly tied blue turban. He speaks in measured tones and is rarely given to raising his voice.

Significant Challenges

However, as Prime Minister there are significant challenges that confront this somewhat genial academic.

Besides the economic and political challenges before the United Progressive Alliance (UPA), whose government Dr. Manmohan Singh heads, there is also the pressing question of framing and implementing policy on improving ties with the nuclear-neighbour Pakistan, and with formulating a view on India's relations with the United States, the only superpower in an increasingly uni-polar world.

On both of the above questions, the previous Atal Behari Vajpayee government has taken significant strides. Notwithstanding the earlier Kargil-conflict, the relations have been on the mend with Pakistan and a series of confidence building measures (CBMs) have been implemented by both New Delhi and Islamabad.

Political Compulsions

The United Progressive Alliance that Singh heads does command the bulk of the Muslim vote in India. It would be at its own electoral peril that the UPA would take any steps to derail the train of India-Pakistan bonhomie, in which the Indian Muslims have an interest.

Prime Minister Singh has committed himself to further improving friendly ties with Pakistan, but a scheduled meeting with Pakistani officials for further confidence building measures had to be "rescheduled" only because there was no Foreign Minister in place in New Delhi long after a very-long-drawn General Elections.

As for the strategic India-US partnership that had been coming about, especially as part of the global anti-terror effort, it may be an entirely different cup of tea.

The UPA government is entirely dependent on the Communist parties for its very survival. The views of the

Communists about western imperialism are well known. Clearly, Dr. Manmohan Singh would need to tread very carefully while working towards building anything like a strategic partnership with the US, even as he must retain the support of the Communists required for running the government in New Delhi.

Pitfalls Ahead

It may be recalled that in months past Washington had been pressing India to send troops to Iraq, as part of a coalition of the willing. India did not accede to the request, maintaining that this issue would be considered once the United Nations sends peacekeeping forces to Iraq. On June 30, 2004, the United States' Provisional Authority in Baghdad may hand over sovereignty to a nominated Iraqi government and the country may have UN supervised elections in early 2005. It will be keenly watched what stand Dr. Manmohan Singh's government would take if and when the question of sending Indian troops to Iraq once again comes up.

Dr. Manmohan Singh's Foreign Minister, Mr. K Natwar Singh, has made it clear that India will weigh several factors before any active engagement with Iraq, for, Iraq is a complicated issue. Mr. Natwar Singh has said that India is glad that the US and Britain have tabled a resolution (regarding Iraq) in the UN Security Council and have come to the US seeking a solution. India has always advocated the involvement of the United Nations in any operations in Iraq..

Mr. Natwar Singh has also revealed that the US has discussed the matter with India and India will "have to see the fate of the resolution they have placed before the UNSC."

Preconditions for Role in Iraq

To play a role in Iraq, India will first see whether the UN resolution is unanimous. It should also be to the satisfaction of the Islamic World and to countries like India that are not in the UNSC.

Mr. Natwar Singh points to the good relations that India enjoys with Islamic countries. He feels that the sooner the situation is improved in Iraq, the better it would be for the world.

It is reported that after Mr. Natwar Singh received a call from the US Secretary of State, Mr. Colin Powell, the US Ambassador to India, Mr. David C Mulford, requested Singh to examine the draft of.the resolution placed before the United Nations Security Council.

Linked to the above is the question of tackling terrorism in India's northern-most state of Jammu & Kashmir. The ruling party in the state is a partner in the Congress Party-led UPA in New Delhi, and its representative, Ms. Mehbooba Mufti, at the very outset demanded an economic package for her state. She has also sought easier movement of Pakistanis to Kashmir.

Soon after Dr. Singh assumed office in New Delhi, terrorists struck in a major way in Kashmir, a landmine blast ripping through a bus killing almost three dozen people, mostly jawans of the Indian Border Security Force and their family members travelling to Jammu from Srinagar.

This tragedy took place just before the first cabinet meeting chaired by Dr. Singh, who condemned the cowardly act of the terrorists in unequivocal terms. A Pakistan-based terrorist group took responsibility for the attack.

Frank Discussions with Pakistan

After assuming office, Mr. Natwar Singh, has advocated "frank discussions" with Pakistan to tell Islamabad that "no positive relationship can be one-sided" and that the new government in New Delhi is looking for a "constructive and creative dialogue" with Pakistan.

The Pakistani leader, General Parvez Musharraf, has invited the Congress Party President, Mrs. Sonia Gandhi, to Pakistan, and Mr. Natwar Singh feels that her visit will help India-Pakistan relations.

The geo-political situation in the Indian sub-continent has undergone a sea change since the Congress Party was last time in power in New Delhi some eight years ago. India's Left parties too have been buffeted by global changes, with Russia becoming an ally of the United States on many issues.

The UPA would need to give a serious thought while framing policies on these and linked issues. Following the rut of a by-gone era will not do. It will require all the genius at Dr. Manmohan Singh's command to bring more than 18 communist, socialist and regional allies that are supporting the UPA coalition to support a common policy that serves the nation's interests on these vital questions.

Political posturing and squabbling would only worsen a difficult situation.

It has been reported by analysts quoting Indian army sources and General NC Vij, chief of the Army Staff that around the time Dr. Manmohan Singh assumed the office of Prime Minister in New Delhi, some 4000 terrorists were poised on the Pakistani side of the Line of Control in Jammu & Kashmir ready to cross the line and undertake terrorist activities in the Kashmir Valley and beyond.

Squabbling Coalition

A squabbling coalition does tie down any Prime Minister, as was reflected in the fact that almost ten days elapsed between the coming in of election results and the swearing in of the government, and in the squabbles over the framing of the common minimum programme as the guideline for the functioning of the Manmohan Singh government.

When asked about the longevity of his coalition government, Dr. Singh told the media that he has faith in the "patriotism" of every member. He felt that "patriotism" would keep coalition partners together and going.

However, to make his coalition more effective and to reduce the damage that internal squabbles between coalition partners can do, Prime Minister Manmohan Singh would have to put in a system of quick response to any rapidly unfolding situation.

The improvement in India-Pakistan ties in days preceding Dr. Manmohan Singh's premiership had a lot to do with the personality and personal efforts of the former Prime Minister, Mr. Atal Behari Vajpayee. The vision and ideas that Mr. Vajpayee had unleashed had caught the imagination of people on both sides of the border, ushering in a new era of friendship even as hardly anyone believed it could be done after the Kargil war.

The Manmohan Singh government would have to come up with a similar effort to continue the process, or else a hiatus can be created which may be detrimental for the improvement of ties between New Delhi and Islamabad.

The recent telephonic discussion between Pakistan President Parvez Musharraf and Prime Minister, is taken a step foreword towards stable peace efforts of India.

The Ex Union Minister for Finance Dr. Manmohan Singh, greeting the Vice President of Switzerland, H.E. Mr. Rene Felber who called on him in New Delhi

The Ex Union Minister for Finance Dr. Manmohan Singh, in conversation with the U.S. Trade Representative, Ms. Carla Hills who called on him

The Ex Union Minister for Finance Dr. Manmohan Singh, in conversation with the Managing Director of International Monetary Fund, Mr. Michel Camdessus who called on him

The Ex Union Minister for Finance Dr. Manmohan Singh, with the visiting President of Uzbekistan, Mr. Islam Karimov

CHAPTER

9

Manmohan's Foreign Policy

Evolutionary not Revolutionary

The new Indian Prime Minister, Dr. Manmohan Singh, faces quite some challenges on the foreign policy front. Without doubt, his predecessor, the Atal Behari Vajpayee-government, did introduce clear shifts in India's long pursued but virtually static foreign policy. Many perceived that under Vajpayee, New Delhi had become quite close to Washington, jettisoning its earlier non-alignment.

The Vajpayee-government, which fought a short-war with Pakistan in Kargil, is also credited with taking huge strides for improving ties with Pakistan, many feel at the prompting by Washington, and succeeding in a great measure.

However, it is said that this emphasis on Washington and Islamabad by the Vajpayee government's foreign policy took away the earlier focus on the SAARC region and on India's extended neighbourhood.

Prime Minister Manmohan Singh has inducted Mr. K Natwar Singh as his External Affairs Minister. The latter is known for adhering to India's traditional foreign policy of non-alignment. Upon the resignation of Vajpayee's National Security Advisor, the somewhat-hawkish Mr. Brajesh Mishra, the calmer Mr. J N Dixit was inducted by the new Prime Minister Dr. Manmohan Singh.

Dr. Singh has committed himself to improving ties with Pakistan and to continuing the process furthered by Mr. Vajpayee for achieving the same.

Kashmir Remains the Stumbling Block

The problem of Kashmir being the stumbling block in this endeavour, Dr. Singh has reportedly gone to the extent of saying that short of secession, short of redefining the national boundaries (in Kashmir), the Indian establishment can live with anything. This indicates that Dr. Singh is quite serious about the peace initiative with Pakistan and for solving the central issue of Kashmir.

In other words, when Dr. Singh rules out the redefining of national boundaries, he also rules out giving any part of Kashmir to Pakistan as part of any deal, maintaining that it would not be acceptable to the Indian people.

Similarly, Singh has also ruled out secession as a solution to the problem, since it would not at all be acceptable to the Indian people. So, there is no independent country called Kashmir in Dr. Singh's scheme of thinking. The Indian Prime Minister adds that such a state would be a hotbed of fundamentalism and would "upset" everything.

So, what is Dr. Singh's solution to the Kashmir problem? Being a thinker and an intellectual, he has thought over this issue and an inkling of his bent of mind is found in his statements.

Soft Borders May be the Key

Dr. Singh believes that "soft borders" may be a way out for solving the problem in Kashmir. He feels that soft borders, that allow people on both sides of the border to move about freely, may hold the key to a solution in Kashmir.

Dr. Singh also feels that a plebiscite in Kashmir would end up being on a religious basis and no Government in New Delhi would be able to survive that, thus ruling it out.

However, Dr. Singh feels that more autonomy for the state of Jammu & Kashmir can be considered through negotiations.

So, the twin-vision of soft borders and more autonomy appears to be Dr. Singh's prescription to solve the Kashmir problem. Prime Minister Singh has said that in case of "soft-borders", the borders are not so important.

Dr. Singh wishes to improve ties with nuclear-armed Pakistan so that both countries can then concentrate on economic well-being of their people. He wants to end all talk of war with Pakistan.

Meanwhile, India's new Defence Minister, Mr. Pranab Mukherjee, has said that the new government hopes to resolve the Kashmir issue through political measures. "But at the same time India has to tackle cross-border terrorism," Mr. Mukherjee has said.

Roadmap for Peace

The new Indian Prime Minister is clearly keen to develop a roadmap for peace with Islamabad. The Prime Minister has the vision of a clear blueprint to re-build relations with Pakistan and other countries in South Asia. Apparently, the priorities of the Manmohan Singh government will be to cultivate good relations, reduce tensions and increase areas of agreement with India's neighbours.

The attitude of India's neighbours also seems positive towards the Manmohan Singh government.. The Bangladesh Foreign Minister Mr. Morshed Khan, visited India to discuss bilateral issues, especially economic cooperation between India and Bangladesh. Also, the Sri Lankan Foreign Minister Mr. Lakshman Kadirgamar, met the new leaders of the Manmohan Singh-government to show Sri Lanka's positive attitude towards India. Sri Lanka would recall the positive Indian role in the Island nation during the time of Rajiv Gandhi.

For establishing better relations in the country's neighbourhood and to assess the situation in the neighbouring countries, the new Indian foreign minister Mr. K. Natwar Singh, just after he took oath of office, met envoys from Iran, Afghanistan and the SAARC and ASEAN countries. He also met with the Indian envoys to the SAARC and ASEAN countries clearly indicating his focus on this region.

Mr. Natwar Singh thus signaled a subtle broadening of India's foreign policy agenda for establishing peaceful relations not only with Pakistan but also with other countries, including China and the Islamic world. Mr. Natwar Singh, first entered South Block way back in 1953 as a career diplomat and went on to become the country's External Affairs Minister. Over the decades, the international agenda has changed in a very effective manner. However, the broad approach, framework and national consensus in foreign policy have survived.

Not Dogmatic

It is clear that India's foreign policy is not linked to any doctrine or dogma and the Manmohan Singh government will take decisions keeping in mind the vital national interests. It may be said that the foreign policy of Manmohan Singh's government is expected to be evolutionary and not revolutionary.

Analysts say that the Manmohan Singh government favours talks with Pakistan on the Sino-Indian model, which provides for dialogue on the disputed border issues without hindering progress in other areas. In any India-Pakistan dialogue on these lines, India would, apparently, not forget Kashmir but would keep it aside in the interests of faster progress on other issues.

The talks mechanism for resolving India's differences with China on the border question was agreed during Late Prime Minister Mr. Rajiv Gandhi's visit to China in 1988.

Meanwhile India and Pakistan are expected to re-start their talks on nuclear and missile related issues. The time taken in the formation of government in New Delhi following the Lok Sabha elections claimed its first set-back on 24th May, 2004, when the high-level talks between India and Pakistan on nuclear confidence building measures (CBMs), originally scheduled for May 25-26, had to be postponed. This was only natural, since there was no government in place in New Delhi, and, consequently, no External Affairs Minister.

The reason behind postponing the nuclear CBM talks with Pakistan was the sensitivity of the subject and it was also important that the two delegations were fully empowered. It may be noted that Dr. Manmohan Singh is very keen to establish smooth and peaceful relations with Pakistan on nuclear and other issues. The new Indian Prime Minister has gone on record to say that he will continue the process of furthering friendly ties with Pakistan.

Focus on South Asia

It is even expected that with the Congress Party-led government, which has assumed office in New Delhi, according a renewed emphasis to diplomacy focusing on the South Asian neighbours, a new dimension would be added to India-Pakistan ties during the premiership of Dr. Manmohan Singh.

When the New Delhi-Islamabad nuclear confidence building talks are held, they will certainly help in building more confidence between the two countries since they will come six years after the sub-continent acquired its overt nuclear profile. Without doubt, these talks would serve the very useful purpose of maintaining communication between the two nuclear neighbours, who have been foes in the past.

Although the ghastly terrorist attack in Jammu & Kashmir just after Dr. Manmohan Singh took oath of office as the Indian Prime Minister was a sobering reminder of the continuing problem, the new government in New Delhi, on its very first day, decided to adopt a two-fold strategy on terrorism. This strategy should also have a bearing on the future talks on the nuclear issue between India and Pakistan.

New Delhi's outgoing NDA government had signed an agreement with Islamabad on 6th January, to take forward their talks also marking the resumption of composite dialogue between India and Pakistan. These talks may establish a solid ground for the subsequent round of talks at the foreign secretary level.

Adhering to the Roadmap

Prime Minister Manmohan Singh has indicated the fundamental continuation of India's security and foreign policy orientation that existed under the previous NDA government. He has also stated that the roadmap agreed between the two countries will be adhered to. The nuclear talks are important because they commit both countries to a framework that will nurture strategic stability between India and Pakistan that declared their nuclear weapons capability in 1998. In 1999, both the countries signed what is called as the Vajpayee-Sharif Lahore Declaration, which recognized the nuclear dimension of the security environment and the consequent added responsibility that this imposed on both New Delhi and Islamabad, especially the avoidance of tension.

India, which is now a major nuclear power, is committed to the policy of "no-first-use" and may be described as the status quo power - in that it perceives the nuclear weapons as having only one purpose - namely to deter the nuclear weapons of a potential adversary. It is expected that India's new Prime Minister will establish better relations with nuclear-armed Pakistan so that the countries can better pursue economic stability and progress.

Pakistani Tactics

On the other hand, Pakistan has tended to behave in the manner of a revisionist power - in that the Pakistani military, which has control of the country's nuclear weapons, has tried to use this capability to seek tactical or territorial advantage or stoke global anxiety by presenting South Asia as a nuclear flash point. The role of the military has always been paramount in Pakistan's politics and President General Parvez Musharraf became the President by using his position as the Army Chief.

In view of this fact, even though the Pakistani government has expressed the hope that under Dr. Manmohan Singh's leadership relations between the two countries will improve and the peace process will continue, there remains the need for a cautious approach. Dr. Manmohan Singh's statement that his government will try its best to establish friendly relations with Pakistan and to talk on all disputed matters, including Jammu & Kashmir, was warmly welcomed by the media in Pakistan.

It is significant that the new Indian government did not request Islamabad to put Jammu & Kashmir on the backburner. In any case, the new Indian External Affairs Minister, Mr. Natwar Singh, has sworn by the Simla Pact signed between India and Pakistan, paragraph six of which talks about a peaceful settlement of the Kashmir issue. If Pakistan makes Kashmir the only agenda for talks, it will be difficult for India to achieve progress on other issues. The two sides need to get over their obsession with Kashmir.

Initiatives Expected on Kashmir

Without doubt, the government of Dr. Manmohan Singh is expected to carry forward some of the foreign policy initiatives of the earlier Vajpayee government, especially in the context of Pakistan. It is even possible that the new government may take some bold initiatives on Kashmir that can work as a twin-balm in both Kashmir and in Pakistan.

However, even as the Manmohan Singh government heads for finding a workable solution to the Kashmir problem, through soft borders and more autonomy, the Indian Prime Minister may win many hearts and minds in Kashmir but the moot question would remain whether any real solution would be acceptable to Islamabad.

Focus on SAARC

Yes, the Manmohan Singh government would put a renewed emphasis on India's neighbourhood, including economic cooperation to mutual benefit, especially in the sharing of river waters, power and other infrastructure resources, as also leveraging mutual advantages of cross border trade.

Mr. Natwar Singh, India's new Foreign Minister, has mooted the idea of common policies in the SAARC countries on security, international relations and economics. If this comes about, it would make SAARC stronger than ASEAN. This could be one significant focus of the Manmohan Singh government.

Mr. Natwar Singh's earlier visit to Nepal, shows the determination of Manmohan's government to improve the relations with SAARC countries.

However, Pakistan's statement aimed at clearing the air on New Delhi's position on Indo-Pak talks, India expressed surprise over Pakistan's objection to remarks made by Mr. Natwar Singh that the Simla Agreement has been the bedrock of Indo-Pak relations.

The question about whether India-US ties still hangs fire. Will the bonhomie with Washington set in motion by the Vajpayee government continue? Or, will it be moderated? Time alone will tell. However, the fact that the communists are supporting the Manmohan Singh-government, and their support would be vital for the survival of the coalition, may well determine the answer to this question.

Defence Minister Pranab Mukherjee - Back at the Helm

CHAPTER

10

Manmohan Singh's Vision for National Security

Even as the Indian Prime Minister, Dr. Manmohan Singh, is a patriot to the core and believes in the patriotism of his coalition partners, the very nature and composition of the coalition government that he leads may have a bearing on India's national security posture.

Demanding Allies

Some coalition partners have forced the repeal of POTA, the legislation to tackle terrorists. Others are apparently out to stymie India's growing proximity to the United States. Still others want India to keep distance from Israel and cozy up to Palestine and the Islamic world.

However, one can glean from the statements made by Dr. Singh, and from his past approach, that he has a clear vision for ensuring national security by solving the problems that confront the country and thus allaying security concerns. It is through constant engagement, diplomatic and economic, with the countries in this region that Dr. Manmohan Singh may leave his mark on improving the country's security situation.

Festering Wound

Take the case of Kashmir, which represents one festering problem that has bedeviled all the 13 Prime Ministers in New Delhi since the days of Pandit Jawaharlal Nehru.

While Pakistan describes what is going on in Kashmir as a "freedom struggle", India accuses Pakistan of sending in armed terrorists from across the Line of Control into Kashmir, engaging the Indian security forces and killing innocents on this side of the Line of Control.

The Line of Control has become the de-facto international border, and Pakistan rules the territory of Kashmir that it took after the incursion in 1948.

Attempts by Pakistan to seek a solution to the problem through the gun has only visited death and misery on the people of Kashmir even as the governments in New Delhi and Islamabad have used up a substantial amount of their treasure over the decades to cope with this issue.

Dr. Manmohan Singh talks of creating soft borders in Kashmir that allow people to cross it with ease. He also talks of considering even greater autonomy for Kashmir through negotiations. If this twin-track approach can abate the problem, it would leave the people, especially the Kashmiris, free to pursue economic prosperity, which would be the best antidote to terrorism.

The problem of Kashmir has been described as the central issue that has soured relations between India and Pakistan. If the Manmohan Singh prescription of soft borders and more autonomy can reduce the intensity of this issue, India and Pakistan can engage each other in trade and economic exchanges in a big way.

One can here learn from the example of Japan and the United States after the dropping of the atomic payload by American pilots in Hiroshima and Nagasaki in the year 1945. If they could get over their past in the interest of their future, why couldn't India and Pakistan?

Economic Engagement

The economic engagement between Washington and Tokyo after that twin catastrophic strike has resulted in a situation that massive American investments are today located in Japan and Japanese investments in America. The cross-ownership and mixed workforce composition of these corporations is such that it is difficult to determine whether the company is Japanese or American. So, if America or Japan were to strike at each other today, it would amount to hitting their own assets. Such a strike is, therefore, ruled out.

If economic exchanges between India and Pakistan, after an abatement of the Kashmir issue, bring the investments of the Pakistani ruling establishment to India and take those of the Indian ruling establishment to Pakistan, the resultant meshing of interests can be the best guarantee for peace. The peace dividend would be higher if these assets are located at target destinations, even if investments are attracted with the help of substantial subsidies.

A Better Bet

In a sense, the approach of having economic inter-linkages with Pakistan is a better bet for peace than that of following the American line in the fond hope that the sole superpower will one day arm-twist Islamabad into desisting from cross-border terrorism or from an attack on the Indian Parliament.

Dr. Manmohan Singh's diplomatic focus on the countries in the Indian neighbourhood with a view to engaging them economically would also go far to strengthen surer, long-lasting ties.

The Common Minimum Progamme, which is the guideline for the functioning of the Manmohan Singh government, is committed to the repeal of the Prevention of Terrorism Act (POTA), which gave law-enforcement agencies sweeping powers of arrest and detention on mere suspicion. It is the considered view of some law enforcement officers that this would dilute the fight against terrorists that threaten the country. But other laws can be used for booking the terrorists, and in any case, POTA had to be repealed in view of its blatant misuse against political adversaries.

The proof of the pudding, however, lies in its eating. It is to be seen if the sincerity of purpose that Dr. Manmohan Singh is displaying would be reciprocated in Islamabad.

To the merit in Dr. Singh's approach, it must be said that there can be no arguments against economic engagement, even with a past adversary. But, as Mr. J N Dixit, the new National Security Advisor, used to say, when dealing with Pakistan one should take one step at a time, with caution. After every step, one should verify the response and then proceed with taking the next step and again verify the response ...

One Step at a Time

One can be sure that the Manmohan Singh-government will certainly take major initiatives on the national security front. The initial response from Islamabad, from none other than Pakistan's CEO General Pervez Musharraf, has been encouraging. But the way forward will be one step at a time, which is the best way to reach any destination.

The focus on economic growth that the Manmohan Singh government stands for, has a positive bearing on the country's national security.

It may be noted that when the Indian economy was floundering in the early 1990s, it was the then Finance Minister, Dr. Manmohan Singh, who took the decision to reduce the budgetary allocation for defence as a percentage of the GDP. While this was implemented as a temporary measure, it has somehow become permanent.

Which means that when the government's deficit is bloating and it is strapped for funds, the budgetary allocation for defence, and consequently national security, can be a casualty. Economic progress thus creates the best environment for greater national security, by making more money available with the government, and by engaging potential adversaries in trade and commerce.

The Manmohan Singh cabinet includes, besides the Prime Minister himself, the Finance Minister, Mr. P Chidambaram, and the Defence Minister, Mr. Pranab Mukherjee, who have been good Finance Ministers of the country.

Without doubt, this constitutes a brilliant trio in the Union Cabinet for addressing the economic affairs of the country. The Prime Minister, the Defence Minister and the Finance Minister, working in tandem, would certainly be able to look at the appropriate budgetary allocations for defence and also create an environment for furthering national security.

Pakistan Back to Square One

A few days after the Manmohan Singh government assumed office in New Delhi, Islamabad test-fired its latest Ghauri-5 Medium-range (1500km) Missile capable of carrying a nuclear payload. The test firing was done reportedly in the presence of Pakistani Prime Minister Zafarullah Khan Jamali.

Around the same time, Pakistan also made a hard-hitting rejoinder to a suggestion made by India's Foreign Minister that the Sino-Indian talks model should be followed for improving ties with Pakistan. Islamabad said that the suggestion had "logical fallacies".

Islamabad has again asserted that the Kashmir issue is "central" and cannot be side-lined. It has said that the

Kashmir dispute is not a border dispute, like the Sino-Indian dispute has been.

A somewhat belligerant Pakistan is asserting that the Kashmir issue can not be "swept under the carpet" and adhering to the Simla Pact, as Mr. Natwar Singh has suggested, would amount to perpetuating the status quo, which is the problem.

Clearly, with the change of guard in New Delhi, and the apparent shift in the emphasis in India's Foreign Policy, Pakistan is once again commencing its rhetoric on a fresh note.

Releasing the Common Minimum Programme
From Left - Dayanidhi Maran, Sonia Gandhi,

Dr. Manmohan Singh

CHAPTER

11

Common Minimum Programme (CMP)

Communists Mount Pressure

The Common Minimum Programme which is to work as a guideline for the working of the Manmohan Singh government was clearly a result of intense pressure tactics by the Communists who have the government by the scruff of its neck.

However, a CMP is better than no CMP at all, and it is to be seen if a deft Prime Minister Manmohan Singh can negotiate his way through this minefield to deliver to the people what they expect from him.

Will the Communists mellow down with time and allow Manmohan Singh's initiatives to come to fruition. Or, will the haggling that went into the making of the CMP stymie normal functioning of the government?

Within days of the Dr. Manmohan Singh council of ministers taking oath of office, the coalition released its common minimum programme, a 24-page document that lays down the guidelines for the functioning of the disparate coalition government.

Finding Common Ground

Considering the fact that the partners in the Manmohan Singh-government have their own policies and programmes, the CMP is a document that attempts to include what is common in the programmes, or election manifestoes, of all parties. It tries to strike a balance in other areas, and glosses over still other points of disagreement. It adopts the strategy of being deliberately vague over contentious issues.

The Communist parties whose support, albeit from outside, is crucial for the survival of the government, played a dominating role in determining the contents of the common minimum programme. It was the leaders of the Congress Party, including Mr. Jairam Ramesh and Mr. Pranab Mukherjee, who first framed a draft common minimum programme for the consideration of the Communist parties who, in turn, made several modifications to the draft. Comrade Sitaram Yechuri was on the three-member committee to finalize the CMP, and in the end, the influence of the Communist parties is writ large on the CMP, even as the Communists have not signed the document. Continuing the obfuscation, Mr. Yechuri told the media, "the Left will endorse the CMP."

As Dr. Manmohan Singh said at the release of the CMP, it "lays down the broad principles that will guide the work of our government."

As if to counter any impression of the conflict of opinions between supporters and partners that the CMP reveals, the CMP itself says that it is itself the foundation of another CMP—"Collective Maximum Performance".

Sonia Calls the Shots

Indicating that she calls the political shots in this government, the Congress Party President, Mrs. Sonia Gandhi, released the document at 7, Race Course Road in New Delhi on May 27, even as all partners and supporters stood in attendance. It was only thereafter that Prime Minister Manmohan Singh read out the salient features of the CMP.

Even though the Common Minimum Programme was crafted in a very short period of time of less than a week, it is a comprehensive document that addresses most issues of vital importance to the country.

The CMP mandates the repeal of the Prevention of Terrorism Act (POTA), which has allegedly been used against political adversaries. It is argued that other laws exist in India for dealing with the terrorists adequately. However, there are those, especially in the law enforcement agencies, who would like strong anti-terrorism laws on the lines of the Patriots Act in the US, to deal with the growing menace of terrorism that threatens the country. One can see the views of the coalition partners from Tamil Nadu reflected in this move where Vaiko, a political entity, has been incarcerated for long under this draconian enactment.

The CMP also promises a National Employment Guarantee Act, which might make the unemployed somewhat happy. But the real solution would be in creating employment rather than in just promising to pass Acts of Parliament.

Addressing the Countryside

When the CMP promises a comprehensive protective enactment for agricultural workers, it is clearly addressing the countryside, in an attempt to further build a base for the United Progressive Alliance, and to be one up on the BJP-led National Democratic Alliance.

The CMP's pledge to increase the public spending on education to 6 percent of GDP has the stamp of Prime Minister Manmohan Singh on it. It is the Prime Minister's vision that nurturing the human resources in the country is the best investment. No country can prosper without its people being educated. However, a cess on Central taxes is proposed for financing this expenditure, which may not go down well with the already-burdened salaried class.

The pledge to "remove communalization" of the school syllabus was only to be expected from a coalition that is painting its political adversaries as "communal".

As regards the privatization of Public Sector Undertakings, the CMP has ruled out the privatization of profit-making public sector undertakings "generally". All privatizations would be considered on a transparent and consultative case by case basis, it has mandated. Clearly, with so many conditions, which private party would put money on these companies? In sum, then, privatization of PSUs is out, without actually saying so, and the Communists have got their way on this score.

At the same time, the CMP has sought to revive industrial growth by boosting private investment and actively encouraging foreign direct investment. It has said that India can absorb, and needs, two or three times the present level of FDI inflow. However, the vulnerability of India's financial system to the flow of speculative capital is to be reduced, as per the CMP. It is not clear where, then, would twice or thrice the amount of FDI come in and get invested.

Reforms with a Human Face

As far as the continuation of the economic reforms is concerned, the CMP repeats the call of the Prime Minister for economic reforms with a human face that stimulates growth, investment and employment.

The CMP commits the UPA government to eliminate the revenue deficit by the year 2009, to release resources for investment in social and physical infrastructure.

On subsidies, the CMP mandates their being targeted sharply at the poor and the truly needy like small and marginal farmers, farm labour, and the urban poor.

The CMP also focuses on encouraging savings even to the point of discontinuing the hitherto policy of slashing interest on bank deposits. It promises interest rates that will give incentive to investors and savers, especially pensioners and senior citizens.

Multi-polar World

On the foreign policy front, the CMP took the Communists' suggestions regarding the multi-polarity of the world and the India's traditional ties with the Arab World and Palestine, but refused to dilute the pro-US stance, or adopt an explicit anti-Israel one.

In South Asia, the CMP mandates close ties with the neighbours, solving of issues with Bangladesh, dialogue with Pakistan on all issues, and support for peace talks in Sri Lanka, the last in deference to coalition partners from Tamil Nadu.

Something for Everyone

In final analysis, the CMP is a document that offers something to everyone, be they coalition partners or various pressure groups in the country being wooed by these coalition partners.

The hectic negotiations that went into the threshing out of the CMP indicate that Prime Minister Manmohan Singh would require all his convincing skills to offer effective governance to the country with the consent of his coalition partners.

It is possible, however, that as time elapses and the coalition partners understand each other's points of view better, they would work as a coherent team to deliver results, if only to retain their electoral relevance.

(The full text of the Common Minimum Programme is provided in Chapter 12)

CHAPTER

12

Text of Common Minimum Programme of the Manmohan Singh-Coalition Government

Introduction

The people of India have voted decisively in the 14th Lok Sabha elections for secular, progressive forces, for parties wedded to the welfare of farmers, agricultural labour, weavers, workers and weaker sections of society, for parties irrevocably committed to the daily well-being of the common man across the country.

In keeping with this mandate, the Congress, its pre-poll allies that include the RJD, DMK, NCP, PMK, TRS, JMM, LJP, MDMK, AIMIM, PDP, IUML, RPI (A), RPI (G) and KC(J) have come together to form a United Progressive Alliance (UPA). The UPA government supported by the Left Parties will have six basic principles for governance.

To preserve, protect and promote social harmony and to enforce the law without fear or favour to deal with all obscurantist and fundamentalist elements who seek to disturb social amity and peace.

To ensure that the economy grows at least 7-8% per year in a sustained manner over a decade and more and in a manner that generates employment so that each family is assured of a safe and viable livelihood.

To enhance the welfare and well-being of farmers, farm labour and workers, particularly those in the unorganized sector and assure a secure future for their families in every respect.

To fully empower women politically, educationally, economically and legally.

To provide for full equality of opportunity, particularly in education and employment for scheduled castes, scheduled tribes, OBCs and religious minorities.

To unleash the creative energies of our entrepreneurs, businessmen, scientists, engineers and all other professionals and productive forces of society.

The UPA makes a solemn pledge to the people of our country: to provide a government that is corruption-free, transparent and accountable at all times, to provide an administration that is responsible and responsive at all times.

Employment

The UPA government will immediately enact a National Employment Guarantee Act. This will provide a legal guarantee for at least 100 days of employment to begin with on asset-creating public works programmes every year at minimum wages for at least one able-bodied person in every rural, urban poor and lower middle-class household. In the interim, a massive food-for-work programme will be started.

The UPA government will establish a National Commission to examine the problems facing enterprises in the unorganized, informal sector. The Commission will be asked to make appropriate recommendations to provide technical, marketing and credit support to these enterprises. A National Fund will be created for this purpose.

The UPA administration will revamp the functioning of the Khadi and Village Industries Commission (KVIC) and launch new programmes for the modernization of coir, handlooms, powerlooms, garments, rubber, cashew, handicrafts, food processing, sericulture, wool development, leather, pottery and other cottage industries.

The UPA government will give the highest investment, credit and technological priority to the continued growth of agriculture, horticulture, aquaculture, floriculture, afforestation, dairying and agro-processing that will significantly add to the creation of new jobs.

Along with vastly expanding credit facilities for small-scale industry and self-employment, the UPA government will ensure that the services industry will be given all support to fulfill its true growth and employment potential. This includes software and all IT-enabled services, trade, distribution, transport, telecommunications, finance and tourism.

The textile industry will be enabled to meet new challenges imposed by the abolition of quotas under the international multi-fibre agreement in January 2005. Given its special ecological importance world-wide and within the country, the jute industry will receive a fresh impetus in all respects.

Agriculture

The UPA government will ensure that public investment in agricultural research and extension, rural infrastructure and irrigation is stepped up in a significant manner at the very earliest. Irrigation will receive the highest investment priority and all on-going projects will be completed according to a strict time schedule.

The rural cooperative credit system will be nursed back to health. The UPA government will ensure that the flow of rural credit is doubled in the next three years and that the coverage of small and marginal farmers by institutional lending is expanded substantially. The delivery system for rural credit will be reviewed. Immediate steps will be taken to ease the burden of debt and high interest rates on farm loans. Crop and livestock insurance schemes will be made more effective.

The UPA government will introduce a special programme for dryland farming in the arid and semi-arid regions of the country. Watershed and wasteland development programmes will be taken up on a massive scale. Water management in all its aspects, both for irrigation and drinking purposes, will receive urgent attention.

The UPA administration will ensure the fullest implementation of minimum wage laws for farm labour. Comprehensive protective legislation will be enacted for all agricultural workers. Revenue administration will be thoroughly modernized and clear land titles will be established.

The UPA government will bring forward a Constitutional Amendment to ensure the democratic, autonomous and professional functioning of cooperatives.

Controls that depress the incomes of farmers will be systematically removed. Farmers will be given greater say in the organizations that supply inputs to them.

The UPA government will ensure that adequate protection is provided to all farmers from imports, particularly when international prices fall sharply.

The UPA government will ensure that government agencies entrusted with the responsibility for procurement and marketing will pay special attention to farmers in poor and backward states and districts. Farmers all over the country will receive fair and remunerative prices. The terms of trade will be maintained in favour of agriculture.

The UPA government will take steps to ensure that dues to all farmers including sugarcane farmers will be cleared at the earliest.

Education, Health

The UPA government pledges to raise public spending in education to least 6% of GDP with at least half this amount being spent on primary and secondary sectors. This will be done in a phased manner.

The UPA government will introduce a cess on all central taxes to finance the commitment to universalize access to quality basic education. A National Commission on Education will be set up to allocate resources and monitor programmes.

The UPA government will take immediate steps to reverse the trend of communalization of education that had set in the past five years. It will also ensure that all institutions of higher learning and professional education retain their autonomy. The UPA will ensure that nobody is denied professional education because he or she is poor.

Academic excellence and professional competence will be the sole criteria for all appointments to bodies like the Indian Council for Historical Research, Indian Council for Social Sciences Research, University Grants Commission, National Council for Educational Research and Training, etc. Steps will be taken to remove the communalization of the school syllabus that has taken place in the past five years. A review committee of experts will be set up for this purpose.

A national cooked nutritious mid-day meal scheme funded mainly by the central government, will be introduced in primary and secondary schools. An appropriate mechanism for quality checks will also be set up. The UPA will also universalize the Integrated Child Development Services

(ICDS) scheme to provide a functional anganwadi in every settlement and ensure full coverage for all children. The UPA government will fully back and support all NGO efforts in the area of primary education.

Proper infrastructure will be created in schools for NCC. NSS, physical development, sports and cultural development of all students.

The UPA government will raise public spending on health to at least 2-3% of GDP over the next five years with focus on primary health care. A national scheme for health insurance for poor families will be introduced. The UPA will step up public investment in programmes to control all communicable diseases and also provide leadership to the national AIDS control effort.

The UPA government will take all steps to ensure availability of life-savings drugs at reasonable prices. Special attention will be paid to the poorer sections in the matter of health care. The feasibility of reviving public sector units set up for the manufacture of critical bulk drugs will be re-examined so as to bring down and keep a check on prices of drugs.

Women and Children

The UPA government will take the lead to introduce legislation for one-third reservations for women in vidhan sabhas and in the Lok Sabha. Legislation on domestic violence and against gender discrimination will be enacted.

The UPA government will ensure that at least one-third of all funds flowing into panchayats will be earmarked for programmes for the development of women and children.

Village women and their associations will be encouraged to assume responsibility for all development schemes relating to drinking water, sanitation, primary education, health and nutrition.

Complete legal equality for women in all spheres will be made a practical reality, especially by removing discriminatory legislation and by enacting new legislation that gives women, for instance, equal rights of ownership of assets like houses and land.

The UPA government will bring about a major expansion in schemes for micro-finance based on self-help groups, particularly in the backward and ecologically fragile areas of the country.

The UPA government is committed to replicating all over the country the success that some southern and other states have had in family planning. A sharply targeted population control programme will be launched in the 150-odd high-fertility districts. The UPA government recognizes that states that achieve success in family planning cannot be penalized.

The UPA government will protect the rights of children, strive for the elimination of child labour, ensure facilities for schooling and extend special care to the girl child.

Food and Nutrition Security

The UPA will work out, in the next three months, a comprehensive medium-term strategy for food and nutrition security. The objective will be to move towards universal food security over time, if found feasible.

The UPA government will strengthen the public distribution system (PDS) particularly in the poorest and backward blocks of the country and also involve women's and ex-servicemen's cooperatives in its management. Special schemes to reach foodgrains to the most destitute and infirm will be launched. Grain banks in chronically food-scarce areas will be established. Antyodaya cards for all households at risk of hunger will be introduced.

The UPA government will bring about major improvements in the functioning of the Food Corporation of India (FCI) to control inefficiencies that increase the food subsidy burden.

Nutrition programmes, particularly for the girl child will be expanded on a significant scale.

Panchayati Raj

The UPA government will ensure that all funds for poverty alleviation and rural development programmes will be credited directly to panchayat bodies as per the recommendations of the Finance Commission. The terms of reference of the Finance Commission will be formulated suitably. Appropriate guidelines will be prepared in consultation with the state governments for the effective utilization of such funds.

Devolution of funds will be accompanied by similar devolution of functions and functionaries as well. Regular elections to panchayat bodies will be ensured and the amended Act in respect of the Fifth and Sixth Schedule Areas will be implemented.

The UPA government will ensure that the Gram Sabha is empowered to emerge as the foundation of panchayati raj.

Scheduled Castes, Scheduled Tribes

The UPA will urge the states to make legislation for conferring ownership rights in respect of minor forest produce, including tendu patta, on all those people from the weaker sections who work in the forests.

All reservation quotas, including those relating to promotions, will be fulfilled in a time-bound manner. To codify all reservations, a Reservation Act will be enacted.

The UPA government will launch a comprehensive national programme for minor irrigation of all lands owned by dalits and adivasis. Landless families will be endowed with land through implementation of land ceiling and land redistribution legislation. No reversal of ceilings legislation will be permitted.

The UPA administration will take all measures to reconcile the objectives of economic growth and environmental conservation, particularly as far as tribal communities dependent on forests are concerned.

The UPA is concerned with the growth of extremist violence and other forms of terrorist activity in different states. This is not merely a law-and-order problem, but a far deeper socio-economic issue which will be addressed more meaningfully than has been the case so far. False encounters will not be permitted.

The UPA government will immediately review the overall strategy and programmes for the development of tribal areas to plug loopholes and to work out more viable livelihood strategies. In addition, more effective systems of relief and rehabilitation will be put in place for tribal and other groups displaced by development projects. Tribal people alienated from land will be rehabilitated.

The UPA government is very sensitive to the issue of affirmative action, including reservations, in the private sector. It will immediately initiate a national dialogue with all political parties, industry and other organizations to see how best the private sector can fulfill the aspirations of scheduled caste and scheduled tribe youth.

Eviction of tribal communities and other forest-dwelling communities from forest areas will be discontinued. Cooperation of these communities will be sought for protecting forests and for undertaking social afforestation. The rights of tribal communities over mineral resources, water sources, etc as laid down by law will be fully safeguarded.

Social Harmony, Welfare of Minorities

The UPA is committed to the implementation of the Places of Worship (Special Provisions) Act, 1992. On Ayodhya, it will await the verdict of the courts, while encouraging negotiations between parties to the dispute for an amicable settlement which must, in turn, receive legal sanction.

The UPA government will enact a model comprehensive law to deal with communal violence and encourage each state to adopt that law to generate faith and confidence in minority communities.

The UPA government will amend the Constitution to establish a Commission for Minority Educational Institutions that will provide direct affiliation for minority professional institutions to central universities.

The UPA will promote modern and technical education among all minority communities. Social and economic empowerment of minorities through more systematic attention to education and employment will be a priority concern for the UPA.

The UPA will establish a National Commission to see how best the welfare of socially and economically backward sections among religious and linguistic minorities, including reservations in education and employment, is enhanced. The Commission will be given six months to submit its report.

Adequate funds will be provided to the National Minorities Development Corporation to ensure its effective functioning. The UPA government will examine the question of providing Constitutional status to the Minorities Commission and will also strive for recognition and promotion of Urdu language under Article 345 and 347 of the Constitution.

The National Integration Council will be restructured and revived so as to fulfill its original objectives. It will meet at least twice a year.

Infrastructure

The UPA attaches the highest priority to the development and expansion of physical infrastructure like roads, highways, ports, power, railways, water supply, sewage treatment and sanitation. Public investment in infrastructure will be enhanced, even as the role of the private sector is expanded. Subsidies will be made explicit and provided through the budget.

The review of the Electricity Act, 2003 will be undertaken in view of the concern expressed by a number of states. The mandatory date of June 10, 2004 for unbundling and replacing the state electricity boards will be extended. The UPA government also reiterates its commitment to an increased role for private generation of power and more importantly, power distribution.

The UPA government commits itself to a comprehensive programme of urban renewal and to a massive expansion of social housing in towns and cities, paying particular attention to the needs of slum dwellers. Housing for the weaker sections in rural areas will be expanded on a large scale. Forced eviction and demolition of slums will be stopped and while undertaking urban renewal, care will be taken to see that the urban and semi-urban poor are provided housing near their place of occupation.

The UPA will pay special attention to augmenting and modernizing rural infrastructure consisting of roads, irrigation, electrification, cold-chain and marketing outlets. All existing irrigation projects will be completed within three to four years. Household electrification will be completed in five years.

Water Resources

The UPA government will make a comprehensive assessment of the feasibility of linking the rivers of the country starting with the south-bound rivers. This assessment will be done in a fully consultative manner. It will also explore the feasibility of linking sub-basins of rivers in states like Bihar. The UPA will take all steps to ensure that long-pending inter-state disputes on rivers and water-sharing like the Cauvery Waters dispute are settled amicably at the earliest keeping in mind the interests of all parties to the dispute.

To put an end to the acute drinking water shortage in cities, especially in southern states, desalination plants will be installed all along the Coromandel Coast starting with Chennai. Special problems of habitations in hilly terrains will be addressed immediately.

Providing drinking water to all sections in urban and rural areas and augmenting availability of drinking water sources is an issue of the topmost priority. Harvesting rain water, desilting existing ponds and other innovative mechanisms will be adopted.

Regional Development, Centre-State Relations

The UPA government is committed to redressing growing regional imbalances both among states as well as within states, through fiscal, administrative, investment and other means. It is a matter of concern that regional imbalances have been accentuated by not just historical neglect but also by distortions in Plan allocations and central government assistance. Even in the Tenth Five Year Plan , states like Bihar, Assam and UP have received per capita allocations that are much below the national average. The UPA government will consider the creation of a Backward States Grant Fund that will be used to create productive assets in these states. The central government will also take proactive measures to speed up the industrialization of the eastern and northeastern region.

A structured and transparent approach to alleviate the burden of debt on states will be adopted at the earliest, so as to enable them to increase social sector investments. Interest rates on loans to states will be reduced and the share of states in the single, divisible pool of taxes enhanced.

All non-statutory resource transfers from the central government will be weighted in favour of poor and backward states but with performance parameters as well. A special programme for social and physical infrastructure development in the poorest and most backward districts of the country will be taken up on a priority basis.

The UPA government will take special measures to ensure that regions of India like in the east where the credit:deposit ratio is lagging, is improved substantially.

The UPA government will review the issue of payment of royalties to states in the area of minerals.

From time to time, previous governments have announced special economic packages as, for example, for the northeast, for Bihar and for J&K. For Bihar, Shri Rajiv Gandhi had announced a special development package in 1989 and subsequently another package was announced at the time of its division in 1999 to make up for the loss of revenue. These packages will be implemented expeditiously.

The UPA government will make the National Development Council (NDC) a more effective instrument of cooperative federalism. The NDC will meet at least twice a year and in different states. Immediately, the NDC will take up the issue of the financial health of states and arrive at a national consensus on specific steps to be taken in this regard. The Inter-State Council will also be activated. All centrally-sponsored schemes except in national priority areas like family planning will be transferred to states.

The UPA government will consider the demand for the formation of a Telangana state at an appropriate time after due consultations and consensus.

The Sarkaria Commission had last looked at the issue of Centre-State relations over two decades ago. The UPA government will set up a new Commission for this purpose keeping in view the sea-changes that have taken place in the polity and economy of India since then.

Long-pending schemes in specific states that have national significance, like the Sethu Samuthuiram project, flood control and drainage in North Bihar (that requires cooperation with Nepal as well) and Prevention of Erosion in Padma-Ganga and Bhagirithi flood control in West Bengal will be completed expeditiously. A Flood-prone Area Development Programme will be started and the central government will fully support flood control works in inter-state and international rivers. All existing schemes for drought-prone area development will be reviewed and a single major national programme launched.

Jammu and Kashmir, Northeast

The UPA government is pledged to respecting the letter and spirit of Article 370 of the Constitution that accords a special status to J&K. Dialogue with all groups and with different shades of opinion in J&K will be pursued on a sustained basis, in consultation with the democratically-elected state government. The healing touch policy pursued by the state government will be fully supported and an economic and humanitarian thrust provided to it. The state will be given every assistance to rebuild its infrastructure quickly. New efforts will be launched to bring investments in areas like power, tourism, handicrafts and sericulture.

The UPA government is determined to tackle terrorism, militancy and insurgency in the northeast as a matter of urgent national priority. All northeastern states will be given special assistance to upgrade and expand infrastructure. The Northeastern Council will be strengthened and given adequate professional support. The territorial integrity of existing states will be maintained.

Administrative Reforms

The UPA will set up an Administrative Reforms Commission to prepare a detailed blueprint for revamping the public administration system. E-governance will be promoted on a massive scale. The Right to Information Act will be made more progressive, participatory and meaningful. The Lok Pal Bill will be enacted into law.

The UPA government will take the leadership role to drastically cut delays in High Courts and lower levels of the judiciary. Legal aid services will be expanded. Judicial reforms will be given a fresh momentum.

As part of its commitment to electoral reforms, the UPA will initiate steps to introduce state funding of elections at the earliest.

Industry

The UPA will take all necessary steps to revive industrial growth and put it on a robust footing, through a range of policies including deregulation, where necessary Incentives to boost private investment will be introduced. FDI will continue to be encouraged and actively sought particularly in areas of infrastructure, high-technology and exports and where local assets and employment are created on a significant scale. The country needs and can easily absorb at least two to three times the present level of FDI inflows. Indian industry will be given every support to become productive and competitive. All regulatory institutions will be strengthened to ensure that competition is free and fair. These institutions will be run professionally.

The UPA government will set up a National Manufacturing Competitiveness Council to provide a continuing forum for policy dialogue to energise and sustain the growth of manufacturing industry like food processing, textiles and garments, engineering, consumer goods, pharmaceuticals, capital goods, leather, and IT hardware.

Household and artisanal manufacturing will be given greater technological, investment and marketing support. In the past few years, the most employment-intensive segment of small-scale industry (SSI) has suffered extensively. A major promotional package for the SSI sector will be announced soon. It will be freed from the Inspector Raj and given full credit, technological and marketing support.

Infrastructure upgradation in major industrial clusters will receive urgent attention.

Competition in the financial sector will be expanded. Public sector banks will be given full managerial autonomy. Interest rates will provide incentives both to investors and savers, particularly pensioners and senior citizens. The UPA government will never take decisions on the Employers Provident Fund (EPF) without consultations with and approval of the EPF Board. Regulation of urban cooperative banks in particular and of banks in general will be made more effective. LIC and GIC will continue to be in the public sector and will continue to play their social role. In addition, the social obligations imposed by regulatory bodies on private banks and private insurance companies will be monitored and enforced strictly.

Labour

The UPA government is firmly committed to ensure the welfare and well-being of all workers, particularly those in the unorganized sector who constitute 93% of our workforce. Social security, health insurance and other schemes for such workers like weavers, handloom workers, fishermen and fisherwomen, toddy tappers, leather workers, plantation labour, beedi workers, etc will be expanded.

The UPA rejects the idea of automatic hire and fire. It recognizes that some changes in labour laws may be required but such changes must fully protect the interests of workers and families and must take place after full consultation with trade unions. The UPA will pursue a dialogue with industry and trade unions on this issue before coming up with specific proposals. However, labour laws other than the Industrial Disputes Act that create an Inspector

Raj will be re-examined and procedures harmonized and streamlined.

The UPA government firmly believes that labour-management relations in our country must be marked by consultations, cooperation and consensus, not confrontation. Tripartite consultations with trade unions and industry on all proposals concerning them will be actively pursued. Rights and benefits earned by workers, including the right to strike according to law, will not be taken away or curtailed.

Public sector

The UPA government is committed to a strong and effective public sector whose social objectives are met by its commercial functioning. But for this, there is need for selectivity and a strategic focus. The UPA is pledged to devolve full managerial and commercial autonomy to successful, profit-making companies operating in a competitive environment. Generally profit-making companies will not be privatized.

All privatizations will be considered on a transparent and consultative case-by-case basis. The UPA will retain existing "navaratna" companies in the public sector while these companies raise resources from the capital market. While every effort will be made to modernize and restructure sick public sector companies and revive sick industry, chronically loss-making companies will either be sold-off, or closed, after all workers have got their legitimate dues and compensation. The UPA will induct private industry to turn-around companies that have potential for revival.

The UPA government believes that privatization should increase competition, not decrease it. It will not support the emergence of any monopoly that only restrict competition. It also believes that there must be a direct link between privatization and social needs-like, for example, the use of privatization revenues for designated social sector schemes. Public sector companies and nationalized banks will be encouraged to enter the capital market to raise resources and offer new investment avenues to retail investors.

Fiscal Policy

The UPA government commits itself to eliminating the revenue deficit of the centre by 2009, so as to release more resources for investments in social and physical infrastructure. All subsidies will be targeted sharply at the poor and the truly needy like small and marginal farmers, farm labour and the urban poor. A detailed roadmap for accomplishing this will be unveiled in Parliament within 90 days. The UPA government will not cut deficits by reducing or curtailing growth of investment and development outlays.

The UPA government is pledged to the early introduction of VAT after all the necessary technical and administrative homework has been completed, particularly on issues like the integration of service sector taxation and compensation to states. It will initiate measures to increase the tax: GDP ratio by undertaking major tax reforms that expand the base of taxpayers, increase tax compliance and make the tax administration more efficient. Tax rates will be stable and conducive to growth, compliance and investment. Special schemes to unearth black money and assets will be introduced.

The UPA government will take effective and strong measures to control the price hike of essential commodities. Provisions to deal with speculators, hoarders and black-marketeers under the Essential Commodities Act will not be diluted in any way.

Capital Markets

The UPA government is deeply committed, through tax and other policies, to the orderly development and functioning of capital markets that reflect the true fundamentals of the economy. Financial markets will be deepened. FIIs will continue to be encouraged while the vulnerability of the financial system to the flow of speculative capital will be reduced. Misuse of double taxation agreements will be stopped. Interests of small investors will be protected and they will be given new avenues for safe investment of their savings. SEBI will be further strengthened. Strictest action will be taken against market manipulators and those who try to deliberately engineer market panic.

Economic Reforms

The UPA reiterates its abiding commitment to economic reforms with a human face, that stimulates growth, investment and employment. Further reforms are needed and will be carried out in agriculture, industry and services. The UPA's economic reforms will be oriented primarily to spreading and deepening rural prosperity, to significantly improving the quality of public systems and delivery of public services, to bringing about a visible and tangible difference in the quality of life of ordinary citizens of our country.

Defence, Internal Security

The UPA government will ensure that all delays in the modernization of the armed forces are eliminated and that all funds earmarked for modernization are spent fully at the earliest.

The UPA will set up a new Department of Ex-Servicemens' Welfare in the Ministry of Defence. The long pending issue of one-rank, one-pension will be re-examined.

The UPA government will make the National Security Council a professional and effective institution.

The UPA government is committed to maintaining a credible nuclear weapons programme while at the same time it will evolve demonstrable and verifiable confidence-building measures with its nuclear neighbours. It will take a leadership role in promoting universal, nuclear disarmament and working for a nuclear weapons-free world.

The UPA has been concerned with the manner in which POTA has been grossly misused in the past two years. There will be no compromise in the fight against terrorism. But given the abuse of POTA that has taken place, the UPA government will repeal it, while existing laws are enforced strictly.

The UPA government will take the strictest possible action, without fear or favour, against all those individuals and organizations who spread social discord, disturb social amity, propagate religious bigotry and communal hatred. The law of the land will be enforced effectively.

Science and Technology

The UPA government will follow policies and introduce programmes that strengthen India's vast science and technology infrastructure. Science and technology development and application missions will be launched in key areas, covering both global leadership and local transformation. The UPA government will mobilize the skills and expertise of Indian scientists, technologists and other professionals working abroad for institution-building and other projects in the country.

Energy Security

The UPA government will immediately put in place policies to enhance the country's energy security particularly in the area of oil. Overseas investments in the hydrocarbon industry will be actively encouraged. An integrated energy policy linked with sustainable development will be put in place.

Foreign Policy, International Organisations

The UPA government will pursue an independent foreign policy keeping in mind its past traditions. This policy will seek to promote multi-polarity in world relations and oppose all attempts at unilateralism.

The UPA government will give the highest priority to building closer political, economic and other ties with its neighbours in South Asia and to strengthening SAARC. Particular attention will be paid to regional projects in the area of water resources, power and ecological conservation. Dialogue with Pakistan on all issues will be pursued systematically and on a sustained basis. The UPA will support peace talks in Sri Lanka that fulfill the legitimate aspirations of Tamils and religious minorities within the territorial integrity and solidarity of Sri Lanka. Outstanding issues with Bangladesh will be resolved.

Trade and investment with China will be expanded further and talks on the border issue pursued seriously. Relationships with East Asian countries will be intensified. Traditional ties with West Asia will be given a fresh thrust. The UPA government reiterates India's decades-old commitment to the cause of the Palestinian people for a homeland of their own. Steps will be taken to withdraw Indian mercenaries from Iraq while further recruitment for this purpose will be banned.

Even as it pursues closer engagement and relations with the USA, the UPA government will maintain the independence of India's foreign policy position on all regional and global issues. The UPA is committed to deepening ties with Russia and Europe as well.

In keeping with the stance adopted by the late Shri Murasoli Maran at Doha, the UPA government will fully protect the national interest, particularly of farmers, in all WTO negotiations. Commitments made earlier will be adhered to, even as efforts are mounted to ensure that all agreements reflect our concerns fully particularly in the area of intellectual property and agriculture. The UPA government will use the flexibility afforded in existing WTO agreements to fully protect Indian agriculture and industry. The UPA government will play a proactive role in strengthening the emerging solidarity of developing countries in the shape of G-20 in the WTO.

Official Language

The UPA government will set up a committee to examine the question of declaring all languages in the Eighth Schedule of the Constitution as official languages. In addition, Tamil will be declared as a classical language.

A Final Word

This is a common minimum programme (CMP) for the UPA government. It is, by no means, a comprehensive agenda. It is a starting point that highlights the main priorities, policies and programmes. The UPA is committed to the implementation of the CMP. This CMP is the foundation for another CMP-collective maximum performance.

CHAPTER

13

Manmohan Singh's Vision of Developed India

Despite it being a crown of thorns that he wears, the new Indian Prime Minister, Dr. Manmohan Singh, clearly relishes the job he is doing.

This is not because he has aspired the loaves and fishes of the high office, but because India's top job gives him the opportunity to translate his vision of a developed and prosperous India that would stride confidently on the world stage into reality.

The last time Dr. Singh got a similar opportunity was in the year 1991 when he became the Finance Minister of the country at a difficult juncture in the history of India, and was able to set into motion unstoppable forces of economic growth. The governments that followed gained from the momentum that he had provided the economy after kick-starting it.

Commentators have stated that Dr. Singh would have liked to have had another term as Finance Minister, after he finished his five-year stint in 1996, to complete the economic resurgence of India that he had so successfully initiated.

Unfinished Agenda

That, clearly, remains an unfinished agenda. The providence has given Dr. Singh the opportunity to complete that task which he had begun in 1991.

Dr. Singh has acknowledged that after India, and a clutch of other countries, all gained independence a bit more than half a century ago, the road to economic well-being that India chose served well only in the beginning, the first few decades. As the decades rolled by, the system itself became a drag on the economic activity in India.

Other countries, meanwhile, went in for free enterprise and empowered their citizens to create wealth through their work, and thus became important players in the world. A country like South Korea even joined the Organization for Economic Cooperation and Development, while India, which was once ahead of South Korea, still grappled with the poverty of its teeming millions.

Dr. Singh, an economic administrator, seems to have found this situation somewhat galling and would like to take corrective steps so that the latent talents of the Indian people can have the opportunity to blossom and India can be a success story, perhaps in one generation.

It is Dr. Singh's desire, as reflected in his statements, that India should once again regain its pride of place on the world stage that this 5000-year-old civilization deserves.

It is also clear from Dr. Singh's statements that he would like Indian economic progress to be rapid and India achieves the developed nation status as rapidly as possible.

Self-belief

For India to progress, Dr. Singh is of the firm conviction that the country cannot depend on other countries. "India has to be developed by Indians, with our own hard work and with our own investments", he has said.

Dr. Singh would like to usher in such economic progress in the country that does not remain restricted to a few people but reaches every nook and corner of the country. The fruits of economic progress must not fill only the pockets of the rich, but must also be enjoyed by the poor and the disempowered.

Dr. Singh would like governance in the country to be a facilitator for development and prosperity.

Dr. Singh believes that the best investment is that in social infrastructure and in human resources. Therefore, his vision incorporates more investment in such areas as health, education, environment and infrastructure that can lead to surer economic progress.

Dr. Singh is all for economic cooperation with India's neighbours for mutual benefit.

At the same time, Dr. Singh would like India to be a global player, to take advantage of the opportunities provided by international trade and the global economy.

Though in his early seventies, Dr. Singh presents a vision of a youthful, confident India, eager to achieve by the dint of its own efforts, much like Dr. Singh has done in his own life.

Inspirational Figure

Dr. Singh is an inspirational figure. The story of his life enthuses one to strive and to accomplish, to be constantly in the pursuit of excellence, to be daring and not diffident, to have faith in the Almighty and to do one's duty come what may.

Fortune, it is said, favours the brave. Destiny must have played a role in giving Manmohan Singh the opportunity to guide the destiny of this great country. In 1991, Dr. Singh would have been happy with a footnote in history. But fate has given him a whole chapter to write as he wishes.

CHAPTER

14

Views from Kashmir

Kashmiris Wish to Remain with India

Prime Minister Dr. Manmohan Singh's association with Kashmir is not new. He was instrumental in the installation of the present People's Democratic Party (PDP)-Congress coalition government in Srinagar-Jammu. The 2002 Assembly elections had thrown a fractured verdict. After a stand-off and failure of various leaders to strike some compromise, it was ultimately left to Dr. Manmohan Singh, as an envoy of Congress President Mrs. Sonia Gandhi and member of the Congress Working Committee (CWC), that an agreement was reached and the first non-National Conference (NC) government took reins in the state after 1975.

He also authored a common minimum programme (CMP) for the Chief Minister Mufti Mohammad Sayeed's government. He was put to service when all the stalwarts of Congress Party's Kashmir Unit, Ambika Soni, Ghulam Nabi Azad and others had failed to consolidate anti-NC forces. These included the CPI (M), a large group of independents, who later formed People's Democratic Front (PDF) and the main parties—the Congress and the PDP.

With this background, from politicians to a common man everybody in Kashmir feels that new Prime Minister has his ears firmly on the ground and he is aware of the nitty-gritty of the Kashmir politics. Dr. Manmohan Singh's assertion that the peace process started by the previous government would continue has raised many hopes. "I will continue the peace process with Pakistan initiated by the previous government and that the process of talks will also continue with the APHC," Dr. Singh said the day after he was elected as Congress-Party's leader.

His statements removed all doubts that the new government will in any way reverse this process. He made it clear that not only the peace process would be strengthened and widened but it would also be carried to its logical culmination. Even more reassuring was his declaration that the process of dialogue with the people of Kashmir would be pursued vigorously and broadened to involve all sections of the people who are willing to join the peace process This is a clear hint that other sections will also be involved with the dialogue started with one faction of the Hurriyat Conference in Jammu and Kashmir.

Kashmiris feel while the new government has removed doubts about its attitude regarding the talks with Pakistan and Kashmiri leaders, it has to move forward with a sense of urgency. Time factor is indeed important. This is particularly so to bring an end to uncertainty and the sufferings of the people.

There are strong vested interests within and outside the country at different levels which would make every effort to derail the peace process or create hurdles in its way. To the credit of Dr. Singh that his resolve remained undeterred despite the deadly explosion along Srinagar-Jammu national highway that killed two dozen BSF personnel and their family members. Many believe, it could have been a message to new government to disengage Kashmiri leaders, who have come forward to settle issues through negotiations.

The "unexpected" debacle of the Bharatiya Janata Party (BJP) led National Democratic Alliance (NDA) at the hustings had come as a rude shock for the moderate faction of All Party Hurriyat Conference (APHC) in Srinagar, who had opted to enter into a dialogue process with New Delhi. They had firmly pinned their hopes on Atal Behari Vajpayee's "realism" and his "understanding" to expedite the process of finding a way-out with the help of backroom American interlocutors. But, Dr. Manmohan Singh's reassurance has rekindled hopes and now the Kashmiri leadership is banking on the "sincerity" of the new Prime Minister.

Moderate faction of Hurriyat Conference has also hailed the new government's agenda for governance. Particularly, they are happy that the decision of United Progressive

Alliance (UPA) government to repeal POTA has created a favourable climate for the future round of talks.

While pledging to respect Article 370 of the Constitution of India relating to Jammu and Kashmir "in letter and spirit" Dr. Manmohan Singh led United Progressive Alliance government has also endorsed the "healing touch" policy enunciated by the Mufti-led ruling coalition in Jammu and Kashmir.

According to the Common Minimum Programme (CMP), the healing touch policy pursued by the State government, will be fully supported by an economic and humanitarian thrust provided to it. The CMP also promised to pursue dialogue with all groups and different shades of opinion in Jammu and Kashmir "on a substantial basis" and in consultation with the "democratically elected" government in the State.

The unilateral categorical commitment to preserve Article 370, though, may not satisfy separatists in Kashmir, but it has paved a way to demonstrate sensitivity towards common Kashmiri sentiments. Prime Minister Manmohan Singh's statement before assuming office that the process of dialogue with Kashmiri leaders will be broadened and taken to its logical culmination had raised the hopes of a realistic approach to the Kashmir problem.

The Kashmir problem has both its internal and external aspects. Externally, Kashmir has been a major cause of conflict between India and Pakistan and a part of the State is still under Pakistani control. The process of dialogue has to be carried at different levels—between India and Pakistan, between India and the people of Jammu and

Kashmir and among the people of the troubled state on both sides of the dividing line.

Internally, the process of dialogue must involve all sections of the people. The colonial policy of "divide and rule", using one section against other, has proved counter-productive in the past. It has only contributed to further estrangement of the people, creating a crisis of confidence. Any dialogue on selective basis, and that too aiming at seeking the approval of the status-quo, is not going to succeed. In fact, this would only strengthen the people's doubts about the sincerity of New Delhi and genuineness of the dialogue process.

Also there is need to have a single centre for pursuing the process of dialogue with Kashmiri leaders. It will be appropriate if it is dealt with at the highest level, directly by the Prime Minister with the help of aides having right perspective and flexible approach. The question of having a separate ministry under the Prime Minister to deal with the special problems like those of Kashmir and North East should be examined with all seriousness.

The CMP talks of implementation of the healing touch policy of the State government, which is committed to release of all political prisoners and putting an end to human rights abuses. Instead of creating obstacles in its way to honour these commitments, the State government should be encouraged to implement its healing touch policy in letter and spirit. The security forces engaged with the task of counter-insurgency should be made to function under a single command headed by the Chief Minister. Kashmiris hope that the new government will address the problem through an integrated approach and bring back peace not only in Jammu and Kashmir but in the entire sub-continent.

There is another view. Noted Kashmiri Pandit leader Ajay Chrangu believes that Kashmir problem can be addressed only by defeating the Pakistani game and the local Muslim communalist forces and lastly to ensure that no group in Kashmir feels discriminated. He maintains that the way new government takes up the challenges in Kashmir will have profound bearing both on Kashmir's future as a secular society and also as a part of India. He says that during the past 15-years, there has hardly been any serious exercise to understand the issues at stake in Kashmir, resulting in the weaving myths to substitute nation-building exercise in Kashmir.

S. Iftikhar Gilani
Bureau Chief (Delhi)
The Kashmir Times
Jammu & Kashmir

CHAPTER

15

What Pakistani Defence Forces Say

The recent change of government in India has come about at a time when there were already definitive signs of upturn in Pakistan-India bilateral relations. Initial statements made by Prime Minister Manmohan Singh and Congress President Sonia Gandhi are very positive and indicate that the direction and tone set by the Islamabad Declaration during the SAARC summit in January 2004, is likely to be maintained. This gives reason for hope that if practical steps are taken to strengthen cooperation at all levels between India and Pakistan, they could transform their bipolar rivalry into a mutually cooperative relationship.

Establishing a Negotiating Framework

The leadership of the two countries should soon seriously engage in identifying a framework for confidence building and resolution of unsettled bilateral issues including the problem of Jammu and Kashmir. The challenge is to anchor India-Pakistan dialogue on to a solid and stable framework that could lead the two countries toward the resolution of issues in a just and equitable manner. And in order to sustain the process of normalization both the government to government and people to people contacts need to progress in an uninterrupted and institutionalized framework.

The forthcoming Secretary level talks should determine the framework of negotiations, the range and prioritization of different items. A multi-speed and multi-track agenda containing positive elements of previous agreements, meetings and summits, particularly those included in the Lahore Declaration and the 1997 MOU agreed by the Secretaries of the two countries could be good beginning It is encouraging that both sides recognize the need for an inclusive agenda. Progress toward the settlement of Jammu and Kashmir is a prerequisite for normalization and will greatly contribute in strengthening a mutually collaborative relationship. Although it may not be feasible to make even progress on all major issues, but from a Pakistani perspective deadlock on Kashmir could derail the peace process. The engagement should avoid media hype, but should be sustained and substantive. Deliberate effort should be made to educate public opinion on the imperative for normalization of relations and to prepare the people that in order to find an amicable solution to the complex problem of Kashmir both sides will have to show considerable flexibility.

Conflict Management

Conflict management is a prerequisite for achieving a durable solution to the Kashmir dispute. The aim should be to eventually evolve a regime for border management that would minimize chances of conflict and facilitate the peace process. The cease fire along the LoC and the international border should continue to hold. Periodic meetings between the opposing force commanders and close contact between the DGMO's has facilitated stabilizing the LoC and should continue in the same spirit of goodwill and understanding. Serious consideration could be given to undertaking additional measures specially the pulling back of artillery and mortars beyond firing range to further stabilize the LoC and give confidence to the civilians to resume their normal lives that have remained shattered for several decades. Agreement on separation of deployed forces from existing positions with a firm undertaking that there will be no forward movement will be another useful CBM. The two sides could also determine certain areas as no deployment zones and agree on limiting forces in areas that are prone to conflict. Both sides could also agree to employing electronic and aerial surveillance in certain selected sectors as a part of cooperative approach in border management. All these measures will be possible if the talks on Kashmir keep moving forward.

As Pakistan has made sincere efforts in curbing cross border insurgency India has to reciprocate by substantially reducing its military and paramilitary forces from Kashmir, which range from 600,000 to 700,000. Reduction of armed forces from Kashmir and improved human rights situation should largely take away the incentive for violent resistance and allow the peace process to move toward a political solution. A verification mechanism has to be introduced to ensure the reduction of forces and prevention of human rights abuses on the Indian side and cross-border movement of insurgents from Pakistan. One possibility might be to use the UN or other neutral observers to monitor the reduction of forces, human rights violations and cross-border violations. By granting access to observers from Amnesty International and Human Rights organizations India will help in easing tension. Prevention of Terrorism Act (POTA), which gives unlimited powers to Indian army and police personnel to summarily arrest, detain indefinitely and interrogate anyone across the board suspected of complicity or allegedly sheltering the insurgents has to be reviewed to make it more humane. New Delhi has to address the legitimate grievances and aspirations of the discontent in populace of Kashmir. Similarly, an understanding for establishing a viable mechanism to monitor cross-border insurgency should alleviate India's concerns. Kashmiris have for decades suffered at the hands of both the Indian security forces and the militants. The attrition caused by the Indian security forces as well as the Mujahideen is taking a heavy toll on the people of Kashmir without clear military or political gains for either side. An enabling environment that gives hope for a peaceful solution is critical for success of the peace process.

Conflict Resolution

Conflict resolution of Kashmir is an essential ingredient of durable peace. Progress on finding a solution would depend on the extent of flexibility New Delhi and Islamabad are prepared to show and whether the two countries give importance to the collective good of the region and the long range benefits of rapprochement. Pakistan lately has shown a great sense of realism and President Musharraf has indicated that he is prepared to go half way.

Several proposals about Kashmir have remained the subject of discussion by various think tanks and policy analysts, but the governments have never formally addressed them at the bilateral level. Among those that have been widely discussed include the plebiscite under the U.N. auspices, conversion of the LoC into an international border, independence of the whole or part of Kashmir, division on the basis of religious or geographical lines, etc. Once the peace process moves forward, the two sides should examine these proposals and look at their feasibility or alternately come out with new ideas and concepts of resolving the conflict. But there has to be sincerity and political resolve to seek an understanding.

Events have shown that even two years after the state elections in Kashmir the Mufti government has failed to establish normalization. Violence, including attacks by insurgents on military targets and repression by Indian security forces continue unabated. For durable peace to be established, New Delhi will have to involve the APHC and its militant groups seriously in any future dialogue. India's policy of putting pressure on APHC to factionalize it would remain counter-productive, as experience has shown in the past. Marginalization of APHC will only breed greater militancy in the state and further hold back any solution of the Kashmir problem. Islamabad could then feel confident and not take sides with any of the factional groups of APHC so that the internal political dynamics could take a normal course and throw up genuine leadership. When India and Pakistan develop favourites among the Kashmiri leadership then the political process degenerates into a proxy power game hurting the real interests of Kashmiris.

Opening the direct Srinagar-Muzaffrabad road link and subsequently connecting a few more cities of the two parts of Kashmir, easing visa restrictions and softening the borders will provide a positive fillip to the peace process. If Kashmiris are allowed to interact then they can also work out what is in their best interest and who can really represent them.

Resolution of allied issues even prior to the resolution of the Kashmir dispute can create a favourable environment and greatly reduce tension between the two countries. This should, however, not be taken that the Kashmiris have accepted the LoC as the solution. Status quo is the problem and unless India is prepared to accept this reality insurgency will not go away. There is a perception in Pakistan that India, taking advantage of the thaw in its relations with Pakistan, will try to further weaken and divide the APHC and impose an internal solution on Kashmir. If peace is to be established in Kashmir, India's policy of internalizing the issue has to give way to new initiatives involving all the three parties—India, Pakistan and the people of the State.

Siachen and Other Issues

Until the recent announcement of cease-fire there were no restrictions on military activity in the Siachen area. There are also no UN observers in Saichen. Troops on both sides suffer heavy casualties mostly due to treacherous weather and accidents. India and Pakistan had twice come close to finding a solution to the Siachen dispute but had to set it aside for political reasons. This issue needs to be reactivated and its settlement could precede the overall settlement of the Kashmir dispute. The proposal for converting Siachen into a peace park can then be jointly undertaken by both the countries preferably with international assistance provided a favourable overall resolution of Kashmir has been achieved.

Similarly, it would be prudent to seriously address the issues of Sir Creek and Wuller Barrage. Sir Creek has given rise to friction between India and Pakistan on matters of territory and limits of economic zones. Both countries continue to arrest fishermen on charges of "trespassing territorial waters" and subject them to great hardships. The matter has also acquired importance due to potential of oil resources in the area. The Pakistani position that the boundary should be along the eastern bank of Sir Creek in the southern coastal area was accepted by the international tribunal. The Indian side from 1966 onwards has claimed that the boundary runs through the centre of the Creek. The delineation of Sir Creek will have to resolve all the major aspects of the problem, which include the land border, the boundary within the Creek and the maritime boundary. Bilateral negotiations should be able to resolve this problem failing which the two sides could agree for international arbitration.

The Wuller Barrage construction was unilaterally undertaken by India in the disputed Kashmir area. Pakistan's objection is that it contravenes the Indus Waters Treaty and will reduce the flow of water adversely impacting on the capacity of dams and generation of hydro-power. Given sufficient political resolve the resolution of all these issues should be possible.

Managing the Peace Process

Keeping the hard-liners in both countries under control would be necessary to prevent them from holding the peace process as hostage. The most effective way of countering them would be to make progress on the issue of Kashmir and simultaneously encourage the development of strong peace constituencies of businessmen, politicians, intellectuals and other segments of the society. Misuse of ideology and nationalism to advance group interests rather than the collective good of the two countries and the region as a whole has to be countered by the governments as well as by the civil society. An encouraging development is that religious political leaders are showing interest in Pakistan - India reconciliation. Main opposition parties in the two countries need to be kept involved, as their support for developing national consensus on major issues particularly Kashmir is invaluable. Mr. Vajpayee had taken certain bold initiatives on Indo-Pak relations. It is hoped that BJP will continue to remain supportive of the peace process.

Role of U.S.

The United States, which enjoys considerable influence in India and Pakistan, has essentially played the role of crisis management by diffusing hostility between the two protagonists. It has, however, kept away from conflict resolution for fear of antagonizing one or both of them. Using back channel diplomacy it persuaded both sides to resume talks. India initially was wary of third party involvement and its insistence on bilateralism has been part of the overall policy to maintain status quo in Kashmir.

U.S. presence has increased significantly in South Asia as a consequence of the events of 9/11, but its current preoccupation with Iraq and Afghanistan and forthcoming presidential elections in the United States are likely to prevent it from devoting any serious attention to the region apart from encouraging dialogue between the two countries. U.S. also realizes the limits to which it can exercise its leverage, as U.S. former Deputy Under Secretary Mr. Talbott once aptly stated: "no amount of diplomatic exertion on our (U.S.) part—on nonproliferation or any other subject—will have much effect unless and until India and Pakistan liberate themselves from their own enmity".

CBMs

With the improved political climate between the two countries it is important that India and Pakistan implement existing CBMs faithfully and develop new ones that generate greater trust and stabilize their relationship. Both countries already have a missile notification program that is by and large being adhered to. There is, however, a need of refining this CBM for establishing greater confidence. For example, they could agree as to how far in advance the notification should be issued. A minimum of seven or ten days advance notice is necessary for building trust. Similarly, they could also include additional details about the trajectory and the duration of the tests. Now that India is developing cruise missiles and Pakistan too is likely to follow, its advance notification should become mandatory and part of the agreement.

High priority should be given to the establishment of Nuclear Risk Reduction Centers to reduce chances of nuclear conflict through unintentional or accidental launch. These centers should have dedicated, secure communication links and should be used for notifying the other side of events on its territory that could be misperceived and lead to a conflict. Other functions for the NRRCs could include exchange of notifications, monitoring CBMs and to supplement other crisis control measures. In view of the great importance of reducing chances of inadvertent nuclear conflict the creation of Nuclear Risk Reduction Centers should not await progress in other areas.

Despite the fact that the two countries have developed long range surface-to-surface missiles that practically cover each other's entire country pulling back Prithvi and Ghaznavi/ Shaheen-1 from forward locations to rear areas will be a positive nuclear CBM.

Nuclear Dialogue

In India and Pakistan the process of doctrinal development has gained pace since the overt nuclearization of both countries. India has now a declared nuclear doctrine which is ambitious in its strategic thrust. Nonetheless, its evolution is likely to depend on the state of its relationship with China and Pakistan and the nation's overall economic growth and national priorities. There is a justifiable fear that India's development of the triad could trigger Pakistan's insecurities and also invite a Chinese response that generates rivalry in the region, creating difficulties in the forward movement of the peace process. India is currently adding to its stockpile of fissile material, moving forward in its land based and air based deployment and gradually working on sea based employment. The "No First Use" Nuclear policy of India does not inspire sufficient confidence particularly since its declaration that if attacked with chemical or biological weapons it would retaliate with nuclear weapons. Moreover, in the absence of a verifiable mechanism the authenticity of No First Use doctrine would always remain suspect.

Pakistan has not formally enunciated its nuclear doctrine although it has spelled out the salient features of it in the form of its non- acceptance of no-first use of nuclear weapons. There has to be an element of transparency in the nuclear doctrine that can help in stabilizing the nuclear relationship between the two countries. Use of common terminology will help in removing misunderstanding about each other's strategic concepts. Indeed, deterrence does require the maintenance of ambiguity in many areas of nuclear operational policy, but development of a common strategic language would facilitate stabilization that could reduce chances of misinterpretation during times of conflict and promote restraint. Understanding of each other's "Red Lines", can have a restraining influence. India's policy is clear that it will respond with massive retaliation in the event of a WMD attack, reminiscent of the U.S. - Soviet model. Pakistani military leaders have occasionally referred to certain "territorial red lines". A major setback to its conventional armed forces can also be assumed to be a critical threshold. A dialogue relating to doctrines can be useful in stabilizing the region.

India and Pakistan could examine further strengthening their nuclear safety systems. They could jointly conduct exercises in responding to nuclear accidents and share experience with each other on safety issues. U.S. may be willing to provide nuclear safety assistance to the two countries.

The MOU signed during the Lahore summit in 1999 had committed the two governments to "abide by their respective unilateral moratorium on conducting further nuclear test explosions", this can be given a legal cover.

It was experienced in the past that during crisis some politicians in the two countries without understanding the full implications of a nuclear exchange make inflammatory statements that only tend to exacerbate tensions.

India's plan to develop Anti- Ballistic Missile Systems is likely to be de-stabilizing for the region, heighten Pakistan's insecurities and could lead to an arms race. This subject needs to be seriously addressed by the two countries in the overall context of strategic restraint regime.

If India increases its conventional forces both qualitatively or quantitatively and alters the existing balance significantly then Pakistan's reliance on the nuclear capability will correspondingly increase thereby lowering the nuclear threshold, however, self destructive this policy may be. For India and Pakistan it is therefore so important for moving from a conflictual to a cooperative relationship to undertake conventional as well as nuclear restraint measures. A mutual balanced forced reduction and pull back of forces from forward areas can be achieved without compromising security. Cooperative politico-security structures will, however, only be possible when there has been significant movement on the political front. It is through a combination of political understanding and a process of arms restraint that India and Pakistan will be able to transform their relationship on sound and stable footing.

Lt. Gen. Talat Masood (Retd.)
Pakistan Army

CHAPTER 16

What Pakistan's Media Says

The first story about the victory of the Congress-led coalition landed in the newspaper offices at around 1300 hours on May 13, and every foreign news agency rushed to get an official reaction from the Pakistan government. A journalist friend had an appointment with President General Pervez Musharraf at 1400 hours and was the first to tell him about the election results and get his spontaneous reaction.

It is said that Congress had not expected to win and Vajpaye had not expected to loose. President Musharraf must have received assessment from the High Commission in India and intelligence agencies to the same effect and was visibly taken aback by the development. However, his first reaction on hearing the news was that with a Congress-led coalition in power, the threat to the process of normalization with Pakistan would come more from extremists like the RSS and the BJP who had subverted the Agra Declaration than from within the Congress party which had supported Prime Minister Vajpayee's initiative. Now sitting in opposition these extremist elements of BJP were expected to take a much more hawkish view of the whole process than before when they themselves were in power.

The decision of Sonia Gandhi not to assume the office of Prime Minister stunned political pundits all over the world but in Pakistan it led the people to enviously point to the difference "here and there." A cartoon in the daily THE NEWS, Islamabad, carried the caricature of three politicians running towards a chair under the caption "here" and "there" she was walking away from the same chair.

Manmohan Singh was not a household name in Pakistan, but the fact that he was the first non-Hindu Prime Minister was highlighted by the Pakistani newspapers who were quick to point out that he was born in a little-known village near Islamabad.

It was due to the reforms introduced by him as Finance Minister from June 21, 1991 to May 15, 1996, that India had transformed from an aid-dependent, inefficient, state-controlled economy into a rapidly developing economy in Asia. A Pakistani commentator was quick to pick up that unlike the finance ministers imported in Pakistan who have worked for donor-driven agendas, Dr. Manmohan Singh seems to be well-versed and familiar with the problems of the impoverished and ordinary Indian folks as Gursharan Kaur, the wife of the Indian Prime Minister, had said in an interview that first thing she would like her husband to do was to hold the price of cooking oil.

He had always been viewed in the official and academic quarters in Pakistan as the Indian equivalent of Dr. Mehboob-ul-Haq, who had started the process of economic reforms in Pakistan and had emerged as a big advocate of a restraint on defence spending in Pakistan, and India.

Dr. Manmohan Singh had served in the IMF and Asian Development Bank. Mehboob-ul-Haq had served in the World Bank. Both were the followers of the free market economy and were for dismantling of barriers and controls. It was as a result of the reforms initiated by Dr. Manmohan Singh during his stint as Finance Minister, continued under the Vajpayee government, that transformed Indian economy into an engine of growth. It was expected that under Manmohan Singh's premiership, the emphasis would be on copying the Chinese and Japanese model of development, under which political disputes are given a back seat and countries concentrate wholeheartedly on the development of international trade and economic potential. This augers well for the prospects of a nuclear and conventional restraint regime.

The process of nuclear confidence building measures (CBMs) had been initiated by late Prime Minister Rajiv Gandhi when he had signed the agreement for not attacking each other's nuclear installations under which the two sides have been exchanging the list of nuclear facilities every year on January 1 for the last 15 years. The talks on CBMs will to be followed by a series of meetings relating to eight subjects that were identified by Pakistan and India in 1997, when a Congress government was in power in India.

With Congress-led government back in power in New Delhi, 'Pakistan government has every reason to feel that the calendar of meetings will remain unchanged. The latest round of talks was to be held by New Delhi May 25-26, 2004. However, hardly 24 hours before the delegation was due to leave, the new Indian government requested the postponment on the ground that a Foreign Minister had not been designated and Indian government was in the process of transition.

The calendar of meetings agreed by two sides in February this year had envisaged meeting of Foreign Secretaries in June this year for talks on peace and security including CBMs , and Jammu and Kashmir. These talks are slated to be followed by talks on Siachin, Wuller Barrage/ Tulbul Navigation Project, Sir Creek, Terrorism and Drugs Trafficking, Economic and Commercial Cooperation, and promotion of cultural exchanges.

The important question being debated by the officials in Foreign Office is if the Indian government would maintain the calendar of the follow-up meetings.

The two most important questions that are to be discussed by Pakistan and India in the meetings ahead are the Kashmir dispute and the nuclear restraint.

Since May 1998, when Pakistan and India carried out nuclear tests they have peddled ambiguous nuclear doctrines and concept of minimum nuclear deterrence. While India has announced its nuclear doctrine, Pakistan has talked about its doctrine but has not made it public. Pakistan government offcials say that the parameters of her nuclear programme are recognizable from the statements of the government leaders and rests on minimum nuclear capability.

However neither Pakistan nor India has spelt out what constitutes the minimum nuclear deterrence.

After the nuclear tests in May 1998, the international communty had urged the two countries to refrain from carrying out additional tests and from deploying and developing them on the delivery systems.

However, just as the international community failed from stopping Pakistan and India from going nuclear, it has failed to stop them from graduating into the next phases, i.e. weaponization and deployment.

Weaponization is the step after the conduct of nuclear tests and consists of the process of developing, testing, integrating warhead components into a militarily useable weapon system. The weaponization system is increasingly complicated and calls for extensive government integration and directions ensuring that the nuclear devices are accident-proof.

The steps involved in weaponsization include:

1. Designing delivery vehicles for the tested weapons;

2. Developing the arming, firing, and fusing mechanisms for the weapons;

3. Conducting environment and delivery tests to ensure that the weapon system would survive harsh and diverse conditions; and

4. Developing handling procedures for the weapon components, assigning responsibility for the weapon components and weapon system with respect to their storage, physical protection and delivery.

Deployment is defined as the process of transferring bomb and/on warheads to military units for storage and rapid mating with delivery system.

Both Pakistan and India are known to have conducted series of tests that aim at testing the range and accuracy of their missile systems. India has conducted scores of tests of missiles that could be fired from land, sea or air and is known to have deployed them in the three services.

Pakistan has conducted at least a dozen missile tests including five nuclear capable missiles, and newspaper reports have talked about the versions that could be fired from the submarine which is under development.

For 57 years, Pakistan has maintained a proportionate expenditure on defence linking it to the Indian defence budget greatly curtailing the fiscal space for expenditure on development and pressing social needs. In 1947, when Pakistan was born, the first budget had allocated Rs.426 million, or 85 percent of the budget for defence. For 57 years, the Pakistan army has maintained a conventional deterrence of one to three against the Indian conventional arms buildup. A senior military official had told reporters in January this year (2004) that Pakistan spent Rs. 184 billion on the nuclear weapons program during 1972-2003 which was more than 7 percent of the expenditure on defence during the same period. This means that Pakistan has spent nearly 2.6 trillion rupees on defence during the same period. Since Pakistan has tried to maintain a ratio of 1 to 3 with India, the expenditure on defence incurred by India comes to nearly 8 trillion rupees.

This means that Pakistan and India has spent more than ten trillion rupees on defence during the last 34 years. No doubt the biggest concentration of the world poor is in the South Asia, particularly the Indian sub-continent.

In his satellite address, arranged by an Indian TV channel, President Musharraf had announced a reduction of 50,000 in Pakistan army but the saving so effected would be used in sharpening the teeth of the Pakistan Army. In fact, the reported reorganization of Pakistan Army is to be carried out as a result of a multi-layer study by a group at the National Defence College. Pakistan Army talks of extraordinary measures to mobilize additional resources to develop its strategic wing.

Both Pakistan and India subscribe to the ideal of minimum deterrence but have failed to define the minimum level of deterrence, an ideal that the United States and the Soviet Union (now the Russian Federation) have managed to achieve in their arms limitation and arms reduction talks.

During his visit to Tokyo in 1998, the then Indian Foreign Minister had told a press conference that India would maintain a minimum nuclear deterrence in two digits but the figure has never been reiterated by any Indian leader subsequently. The race for maintaining the strategic edge between the two countries continues as brought into sharp focus by the test-firing of missiles.

Pakistan has set up the nuclear command and control authority (NCA) as the principal strategic policy maker while Strategic Plans Division (SPD) headed by a Lt. General, and Army Strategic Force, commanded by another Lt. General, has been constituted. There is also talk of setting up strategic force in navy and air force as well.

Speaking at the firing of Hatf-V missile from an unspecified place, Prime Minister Zafarullah Khan Jamali declared that "Pakistan's edge over its adversaries in the strategic field will be maintained at all costs and his government will provide necessary resources to maintain the quality of the nation's deterrence." This means that the modernization of the missiles and miniaturization of the nuclear devices would continue.

Pakistan's economic, foreign and security policies have been India-specific. They were best summed up by President Ayub in a conversation with the US ambassador Mcnaughy at the height of tension with India, as recently revealed by the declassified American documents.

"Pakistan would be willing if necessary to be a satellite of the US if she remains secure from India. But we can never accept a relationship which would expose us to be satellite of India", Ayub had said.

Pakistan-India relations have been governed by Newton's third law of force that "to every action there is an equal reaction in the opposite direction." The amount of money that India would pour in building up its defence muscle would determine the amount to be allocated by Pakistan. In the process the wheels of poverty would plunge the impoverished people of the Indian sub-continent into a deeper quagmire.

The experts on Nuclear CBMs are expected to meet two days before the Foreign Secretaries meeting in June this year and would take up a Pakistani proposal of nuclear and conventional restraint in the region which should include a definition of the minimum nuclear deterrence. The comments in the Indian newspapers, as for example, by Raja Mohan in the *Hindu* dated May 23, 2004, indicate that India regards it as a Pakistani ploy to bridle Indian strategic designs.

The million dollars question agitating the minds of the policy makers in the Foreign Ministry is if the memorandum of understanding signed by Foreign Secretaries of Pakistan and India in February 2001, in Lahore would be the basis of Nuclear CBMs or like the proverbial Pathan, the two sides would wipe the slate clean and start from zero once again!

Would Pakistan-India take the thread from Simla Accord or the Lahore Declaration?

Will the new National Security Advisor J.N.Dixit begin a new round of talks or will the two sides make capital out of the efforts that have been made by Pakistani interlocutors like Tariq Aziz and Niaz Naik in their backroom diplomacy with the former Indian National Security Advisor Brajesh Mishra?

Shahid U R Rehman
Senior Journalist, Pakistan and
Staff Correspondent
Kyodo News Agency (Japan)

CHAPTER

17

India-US Ties

Rhetoric Won't Derail Them

The coming to power of the Dr. Manmohan Singh government in New Delhi marks a complete change on the political canvas of the country. For the first time in the history of the Indian Republic, the Indian Communists are calling the shots in framing New Delhi's policies, especially the foreign and the economic policies.

Indian Communists' Role

This dominant role of the Communist parties is sure to impact the relations between New Delhi and Washington, which have seen a remarkable improvement in recent years.

While the whole world acknowledges that communism is now virtually a part of history, that the erstwhile Soviet Union is a thing of the past and that the United States is the sole superpower, the Indian Communists, even after the formation of Manmohan Singh government, continue to harp on the multi-polarity of the world. This is seen as a manifestation of the continued animosity of the Indian Communists towards the West in general and the United States in particular.

The Communist Party of India (Marxist)'s Prakash Karat has gone to the extent of demanding that the "tilt" in India's foreign policy towards Israel "must end" and that India "has to sympathize with Palestine".

US Should Leave Iraq, say Communists

Even as some 1,38,000 US troops, and some 9,000 British soldiers, occupy Iraq, the Indian Communists are swearing by India's traditional friendly ties with the Islamic world and the Arab world, India's traditional support for Palestine as also censure of Israel, even as they demand that the US vacate Iraq.

On the economic front too, the Indian communists are harping on discouraging "speculative" foreign direct investment.

However, the Congress Party, which does not see eye-to-eye with the Indian Communists on these issues, would resist actually spelling out policies in tune with the desires of the Communists. However, the Manmohan Singh government might find it difficult to implement foreign policy that leans more towards the United States as the Communists keep him engaged in unending arguments and negotiations.

The Congress Party had been out of power in New Delhi for eight long years before the inauguration of the Manmohan Singh government. And, the Indian Communists are seen to perpetually live in the past and still draw their inspiration from Marx and Lenin. In recent years, the world has changed drastically, and so has India's foreign policy adjusted itself in tune with the changing times.

It may be remembered that ageing stalwarts of the Congress Party too have been fascinated by Nehru's concepts of Panchsheel and Non-alignment, and would find it hard to jettison these ideas at the fag end of their lives and careers and may not endorse a tilt towards the United States.

Body Blows to Policy

The combination of the Indian Communists and the gray-haired Congressmen can deliver body blows to the new-found pragmatism in India's foreign policy, that has been adapting itself to suit the country's best interests, rather than sticking to any dogma.

Pragmatic foreign policy is crucial to the security policy of any country. This has been exemplified in India's apparent US-tilt in foreign policy putting pressure on Pakistan to curb cross-border terrorism. What use is a predictably dogmatic foreign policy that can harm a country's security interests, by allowing its adversary with a more flexible foreign policy to gain favours from the sole superpower?

It is being speculated that the changes which the Manmohan Singh government may have to make to the country's policy towards Washington, under pressure from its coalition partners, may also impact the nation's security scenario.

While India's Communist Parties are perceived to be anti-US, the Congress party has also described in its pre-election document that the BJP government reduced India "to a sub-ordinate relationship with the United States where the latter takes India for granted."

Whither India-US Partnership?

If that be the stand of the Manmohan Singh government, it can put paid to any hope of a strategic security partnership between New Delhi and Washington. This may, in turn, allow Islamabad the opportunity to be the sole friend of the US in this region, and get all the favours that go with that position.

Mr. Prakash Karat, who is a CPI(M) Politbureau member, advocates a "course correction" in the foreign policy pursued by the previous NDA government headed by Prime Minister Atal Behari Vajpayee.

Karat criticizes the Vajpayee government for tying India's foreign policy to the strategic goals of the United States and demands that India should revert to its earlier "independent foreign policy". Karat wants India not to be seen as the Chief Agent of the United States in South Asia and also wants an end to the US occupation in Iraq.

What the Communists are thus seeking is a complete reversal of the recent Indian tilt towards the US, and in fact, injecting an anti-US element in India's foreign policy.

Another casualty of the Indian Communists' dictating of India's foreign policy may be India's participation in the global war against terror, and of the benefits that India has drawn from this participation. India's proximity to Israel was initiated when Congress Party's P V Narasimha Rao was the Prime Minister of the country. It was when the US also became a victim of the global Islamic terror network, that India, Israel and the US - all victims - commenced their cooperation on this front, sharing intelligence, holding exercises and working in tandem.

Natwar Singh: Close Relations with US

However, India's new Foreign Minister, Mr. K Natwar Singh, is categorical in stating that his government is for "the closest relations with the United States." How the Prime Minister will reconcile what Mr. Natwar Singh says with what Mr. Praksh Karat says remains to be seen.

Consequences of one's actions are said to be the best teachers. The consequences of toeing the Prakash Karat line in India's foreign policy may well be catastrophic, not only frittering whatever advantages the country may have gained, but putting New Delhi in the direction of isolation from the global mainstream. If that happens, it would be a sad case of India missing the global bus once again, as in the 1950s and 1960s, which had terrible economic consequences for the country. We had chosen Non-alignment then, and the other similarly placed countries, including South Korea, achieved stunning economic progress after adopting a more flexible economic and foreign policy.

However one must be cautious in jumping to any conclusion about the final stand and should look at the Indian Communists' anti-US posturing in greater detail. What prompts it? In part, this attitude can be explained by the books that these Marxists and Leninists have read in their early and later lives, which keep them from seeing the world as it really is, and their propensity to speak to the press at the drop of the hat.

But there is another explanation to this anti-US posturing by the Indian Communists.

The Indian Communists are not impractical people. They have quite often wielded power in New Delhi disproportionately greater than their numbers in Parliament have justified. Much though they might rail against Parliamentary Democracy, they remain creatures of India's electoral politics, which is the road to power.

Communists' Compulsions

Even as the United States of America is perceived as anti-Islam worldwide, the Indian Communists realize that opposing the United States is the best way to get the Muslim voter on their side in India. This makes good political sense and may be the real reason for the Indian Communists' continued stand against the United States.

If this is indeed the case, there remains an opening for the new Indian Prime Minister and the new Indian Foreign

Minister to continue to improve relations with Washington. This can happen so long as a song and dance is not made of the improvement of ties with the United States. The Indian Communists should not be embarrassed before their Muslim voters, even as American investments continue to be welcome in the country.

No Setback to India-US Ties

Clearly, one has to sift through the rhetoric to grasp which direction the India-US ties will take under the Manmohan Singh government. It is quite possible that the anti-US statements and posturing might continue, but substantively the things may remain much the same, or even improve, the more they appear to be worsening.

CHAPTER

18

Foreign Media Welcomes Dr. Manmohan Singh

Dr. Manmohan Singh deserves the highest post in India and will prove to be the leader India needs at this critical juncture.

It will not be easy for him, since he has inherited a pile of tasks and responsibilities. He would need internal stability, healing touch, harmonious coexistence to take further the economical reforms and provide political stability. Dr. Singh's clean image will ease his tasks a bit as he is modest in his approach and capable of dealing with both friends and foes, a true believer, a devoted family man and above all loyal to his party and its leadership. It makes him the ideal choice for the post. Dr. Manmohan Singh is an open minded, good listener and ready to apply his mind and soul whenever needed and a good advisor whenever he is asked for his opinion.

Whenever Dr. Singh attends an official party he never makes noises. He comes and goes very quietly. If you look into his face, you will be able to see a kind of quality he possesses and you will come to respect the man.

His qualities have gained him the respect from Indian and international media, which was more candid and a bit critical of his personality. He will prove even to his critics that he is the politician with no personal ambition to rule the country. He is only interested in delivering the goods to his nation. Though many will argue that he is more popular among middle class Indians because of his consumer-friendly policies that helped the consumer class to flourish when he was a finance minister. But Dr. Singh of the nineties is different now and his economic decisions will be more friendly to all strata of the Indian society particularly to the weaker class to improve their socio-economic conditions.

It is easy to prescribe the medicine once you diagnose the illness but Dr. Singh enjoys both and he will be in a position to prove his mettle and implement his policy with consensus and, of course, with his vision. He will not face much challenges from his partners who know that the prime minister is doing good for the country's future.

Dr. Singh no doubt belongs to the old guard but his ability to learn quickly and understand the needs and apply the correctives will make him more popular among his third generation countrymen. This is a rare combination of a leader in contemporary history.

He is more ambitious now to leave his mark in Indian history as the chosen one for the job. His early childhood trauma of partition and its fallout on millions of families on both sides of the border will help him work towards removing boundaries among neighbuors, specially with Pakistan. Increasing economic relations and people to people contact will help in providing security and stability in the region.

He will be remembered for years to come if he is allowed to function smoothly.

Mrs. Sonia Gandhi had no difficulty in picking him for the job for the kind of quality and reputation he enjoys. She is more lucky because he belongs to the Sikh community and she will be able to bank on him. With his kind of leadership the Congress Party will gain its lost glory and he will pave the way for the young Turk in the Party to take over and lead the country as a strong democratic nation, with its multi cultures, ethnic, religious and secular outlook. Dr. Singh is aware of his task and responsibility and he is capable of shouldering it. He is no spoiler but rather a true server, eager to do whatever is required to serve his country and the nation.

Dr. Waiel Awwad

President of Foreign Correspondents Club of South Asia (FCC), New Delhi, and Alarabiya South Asia Bureau Chief.

CHAPTER

19

Plans and Views of Prime Minister's New Team

The important leaders of newly formed Dr. Manmohan Singh's government have assured the country that they want to take it faster on path of growth, development and provide social equity. Some excerpts from their statements are given here to illustrate their views .

Mr. P. Chidambaram: Finance Minister

It is expected large that there will be a renewal of reforms due to the return of Mr. Chidambaram. He is called the "darling" of corporate India. The surprise announcement of the finance portfolio for Mr. Chidambaram, earlier expected to be kept by the Prime Minister Dr. Manmohan

Singh himself, is a clear indication that the Congress-led UPA government will vigorously pursue economic reforms aimed at achieving high growth and better living standards for the public. The finance minister has the best pro-market reforms credentials, perhaps only next to the Prime Minister Dr. Manmohan Singh, known all-over the world as the architect of India's economic reforms. Both were in the Narasimha Rao government when it took over in 1991 in the midst of a severe economic crisis. Mr. Chidambaram was the commerce minister while Dr. Singh was the finance minister.

In some way, the credit for initiating the reforms could be given to Mr. Chidambaram as the India's inwardlooking trade policies of the 60s and 70s were the first to go. Within a week of the Rao government taking office, Mr. Chidambaram announced radical and dramatic trade policy reforms starting off the process of deregulation and liberalisation. In fact, when the pace of economic reforms slowed down after the Narasimha Rao government met with electoral debacles in states like Karnataka and Andhra Pradesh, it was Mr. P. Chidambaram who kept urging for faster reforms and thus, acquired the image of an "ultra-re-former". But Mr. Chidambaram's reforms credentials were best established when he took over as the finance minister of the United Front government, which had the support of the left parties from both inside and outside the government. Mr. Chidambaram, who in his student days was an activist of the CPM's student wing, SFL, but began his political career in Congress, had moved out to form a regional outfit, Tamil Manila Congress. He played a leading role in drafting the common mimumum programme (CMP) of United Front government, which broke new grounds with regard to disinvestment of public sector enterprises.

Mr. Chidambaram presented two market and middle class-friendly budgets which pushed economic reforms in key sectors of the economy including agriculture and infrastructure. The budget for 1997-98, billed as a "dream budget", introduced far-reaching tax reforms firmly based on the principles of modernisation and minimisation of tax rates and voluntary compliance. A voluntary disclosure of income scheme (VDIS) during his time was hugely successful, and brought out an estimated Rs. 50,000 crore of black money into the system and earning a revenue of Rs. 10,000 crore.

New Agenda of Finance Minister

Agriculture

* Priority would be given to agriculture,
* Rural credit to be doubled in three years,
* Controls on farmers to be lifted,
* Irrigation projects to be completed in 3-4 years.

Industry

* Priority to develop and expand ports, airports, water and sanitation projects,
* Public and private investments to be encouraged in infrastructure,

* Bigger share for corporates in power generation and distribution,

* Unbundling of SEBs postponed till consultations are held,

* Encourage public and private partnership in core sectors.

Foreign Investment

* $ 10-15 billion annual foreign investment flows targeted,

* Foreign investment to be encouraged in infrastructure, high technology and exports,

* FDI in airports yet to be finalised.

Public sector

* Banks to enjoy complete managerial and commercial autonomy,

* Small investors to be allowed new safe investment avenues,

* Strike a balance between interest rates on savings and borrowings.

K. Natwar Singh: Minister of External Affairs

In his press conferences after assuming office, Mr. Natwar Singh has stated that relations with China and the Islamic world were as much a priority for India as ties with the US. He signalled a subtle broadening of the country's foreign policy agenda. Recalling that he entered South

Block first time in 1953, he noted, "India has changed, the world has changed, we have changed. The international agenda has changed". However, the broad approach, framework and national consensus in foreign policy has survived (all) these years, he said.

Though he traced the foundations of Indian foreign policy to Nehru's intervention at the 1927 Brussels Conference of Oppressed Nationalities and the 1938 Haripura Congress session where "Pandit Jawaharlal Nehru said that India would not be with either the capitalist or communist camp", Mr.Natwar Singh avoided any reference to non-alignment or NAM in his quick recounting of foreign policy priorities. Also missing was any reference to India's relations with Israel, something the NDA government frequently spoke of. It suggests that while there will be a reassessment of India's foreign policy on one or more key fronts, the Ministry of External Affairs (MEA) under him will continue to deal with the world as it exists rather than seeking to resurrect old solidarities which perhaps no longer exist. "India's foreign policy is not linked to any doctrine or dogma", said Mr. Natwar Singh, "and we take decisions keeping in mind our vital national interests."

Mr. Natwar Singh favours talks with Pakistan on the China-India model which provides for dialogue on the complex border issue without hindering progress in other areas. "Why don't we follow the same example since Pakistan is close to China and so is India. We are saying that do not forget issue of Kashmir but keep it aside for faster progress on other disputes". Mr. Natwar Singh said he was not asking Islamabad to put Kashmir on the backburner because sixth paragraph of the Simla Agreement talked about a peaceful settlement of the issue. But if Islamabad makes Jammu & Kashmir the only agenda, then the smooth talks and relations may not be possible. Both sides needed to get over their obsession with Kashmir. On Israel, he said, "India is quite clear that our relations with Israel will not be at the cost of the legitimate aspirations of the Palestinian people, which we will support'.

The minister said that India's differences with Beijng on the border question - the dialogue mechanism for which was agreed during Rajiv Gandhi's 1988 visit to China - had not impeded our relations in other areas. Talking on a bunch of issues, Mr. Natwar Singh said that he had told the US secretary of state Colin Powell that his government had "hit the road running" in the area of foreign policy. "We welcome the improvement in relations with the USA. India will carry it forward, deepen it, widen it and strengthen it."

Pranab Mukherjee: Defence Minister

Will the new government use the recently signed defence deals to haul the previous BJP-led NDA regime, especially former defence minister Mr. George Fernandes, over the coals? Will some more skeletons now tumble out of the defence cupboard? These were the questions doing the rounds of South Block. Though Mr. Mukherjee himself did not say so in as many words, he did indicate that the government would "look into" the defence deals concluded by the previous regime if "any specific alligations" came up.

In a clear swipe at the NDA government, he stressed his endeavour would be to make the entire defence procurement process, both for regular and emergency requirements, "more clear and transparent". Congress, in fact, had vehemently attacked the NDA government for obfuscating the Tehelka, Coffin and other defence scams. The changeover in the defence ministry clearly has made some senior officials jittery. Although the minister said that he did not hope there was any unnecessary witch-hunt since it would hit the already painfully slow decision-making here. The last NDA government had, incidentally, signed a flurry of mega deals in the run up to the April-May elections. These included the Rs. 6,900 crore Russian aircraft carrier Admiral Gorshkov package deal on January 20, the Rs. 8,000 crore British `Hawk' advanced jet trainer (AJT) project on March 26, and the Rs. 5,000 crore Israeli `Phalcon' early-warning radars for the AWACS programme on March 5. On his part, Mr. Mukherjee said that the new government would strive to eliminate all delays in the modernisation of the armed forces by ensuring that all budgeted funds for new weapon systems were fully utilised. He said that it is plain and simple "bad management" when the country is not able to modernise its armed forces despite availability of funds. He took pains to refute the "soft-on-national security issues tag", which the much more hawkish BJP has often pinned on Congress. He said, Congress had always had a bold and consistent stand on issues connected with the country's security.

Shivraj V. Patil: Home Minister

Mr. Shivraj Patil said that India is ready to talk to everyone, but the government should not be taken as weak or soft. The newly elected UPA government will adopt a "carrot-and-stick" approach in dealing with militants and separatists in Jammu and Kashmir and insurgent groups in the North-East. Mr. Patil said there was "no question of not talking to our breathren" and "bringing them back on the right path". At the same time, he made it clear that terrorism, in whatever form, would be met squarely and firmly. "Our endeavour would be to control and eliminate terrorism... We would like to see the law taking its own course," he said. When it was asked if the killing of BSF personnel and their family members in a landmine blast in Kashmir on 23rd May, 2004, was timed to coincide with the first day in office of the Manmohan Singh government, Patil remarked, "India is too big a country", which amounted to being non-committal. Of course, Patil promptly visited the wounded jawans in hospital.

On whether he considered Naxalites and other Left extremist groups as political movements or merely a law-and-order problem, he said they were "movements that need to be tackled properly. We need to tackle the problems of the people of the area. We can think of an economic package for these areas. Dialogue is important, but how it is done needs to be carefully determined. The Andhra Pradesh government's dialogue with the People's War Group would go on while the Union government adopts a national, multi-pronged approach towards the extremists. "Police action is one thing, solving economic problems (of areas where these groups operate) is another," Mr. Patil said.

Praful Patel: Civil Aviation Minister

Will domestic airlines go west? There's good news ahead for India's private domestic carriers Air Sahara and Jet Airways. The new civil aviation minister said after assuming office that the Congress-led coalition government is keen on allowing private domestic airlines to fly on more international routes. The last NDA government had proposed to allow them to operate flights across the globe, except to the Gulf countries. However, the proposal was deferred at the NDA's last cabinet meeting following stiff opposition from Mr. Arun Shourie and a few other cabinet ministers. "India wants more capacity to be made available for our international travellers. The priority will be to strengthen Air-India so that it can provide this connectivity. The remaining sectors will be divided among the other domestic players. It is better than allowing a foreign carrier to come in and take away our traffic," Mr. Patel said after taking charge as the civil aviation minister.

The new government, he said, would also continue the restructuring exercise of Delhi and Mumbai airports that was initiated by the NDA government. However, sources pointed out that the process of inviting expression of interest (EoI) from global developers will be delayed slightly.

HR Bharadwaj: Law Minister

Mr. Bhardwaj took over the third time as the law minister on 24th May, 2004. He promised repealing or amending the anti-terror law POTA, and stated that the rule of law would prevail everywhere including Gujarat, vacancies in high courts would be filled and that fast track courts would not be touched. He also extended a friendly hand to the judiciary by stating that there would be no National Judicial Commission since it is an "unrealistic" idea. "NJC has been a non-starter from the day one." The minister said that the government is not interested in pursuing it. Instead, he would talk to the Bench and bar to evolve a harmonious relationship'. The minister also promised to investigate why there are so many vacancies in the high courts. He said, "if the vacancies are filled, the backlog of cases would come down dramatically". He assured that his ministry would come out with a charter of reforms soon with an emphasis on speedy justice. When there was a mention of a scandal in the judiciary, Mr. Bharadwaj paused. But it barely lasted a second. It is not a happy situation. "He said that he would talk to the Chief Justice of India as to how to improve the shoddy image of the judiciary".

Kamal Nath: Commerce and Industry Minister

What is the agenda of the new minister of Commerce and Industry? Will the new government boost exports by focusing on the Exim Policy? The centre proposes to do away with controls on exports, cut delays and enable exporters to reduce transaction costs. Removing delays in procedures will be the focus of the new Exim policy. While addressing exporters in his first interaction, Mr. Kamal Nath gave a firm indication to this effect.

Special emphasis in the new Exim policy would be on agriculture and services sectors, the minister hinted. Apart from these, agro and processed food, minor forest products would also get a big push to create employment opportunities in backward areas, he added. The minister said that "we must aim to make India a hub of manufacturing as well as services for the rest of the world". It may not be possible unless transaction costs are brought down to the bare minimum, he added. "Our country intends to focus on reorientation of our delivery systems and restructuring the existing organisation for expanding the country's manufacturing and services in general and exports in particular", he emphasized. The exporters asked the minister to take up the issue immediately with the finance minister Mr. P. Chidambaram. They also asked the minister to prevail upon the finance minister to make available dollar loans at Libor plus basis so that exporters could get immediate relief. The Federation of Indian Exporters Organisation (FIEO), in its pre-exim policy memorandum, has also asked the centre to provide a fiscal incentive package to boost exports from small scale, cottage and tiny sectors as they provide large employment. The president of FIEO suggested that various taxes paid by small and medium exporters should be reimbursed.

Left: The Ex Union Minister for Finance Dr. Manmohan Singh,
giving final touch to the Union Budget
Right: He is arriving to present the Union Budget for the year 1991-92

PM, Dr. Manmohan Singh with Finance Minister Chidambaram

CHAPTER

20

Profile of Dr. Manmohan Singh
Prime Minister of India

Academic Record

1962	D. Phil., Nuffield College, University of Oxford, Topic: India's Export Trends and Prospects for Self-Sustained Growth. [Published by Clarendon Press, Oxford, 1964]
1957	Economic Tripos [First Class honours], University of Cambridge
1954	M.A. Economics, Panjab University - First Class with first position in the University
1952	B.A. Economics (Hons.), Panjab University - Second Class with first position in the University

1950 Intermediate, Panjab University - First Class with first position in the University

1948 Matriculation, Panjab University - First class

Prizes and Awards

2000 Conferred Annasaheb Chirmule Award by the W.G. alias Annasaheb Chirmule Trust set up by United Western Bank Limited, Satara, Maharashtra.

1999 Received H.H.Kanchi Sri Paramacharya Award for Excellence from Shri R. Venkatraman, former President of India and Patron, The Centenarian Trust

1999 Fellow of the National Academy of Agricultural Sciences, New Delhi.

1997 Conferred Lokmanya Tilak Award by the Tilak Smarak Trust, Pune

1997 Received Justice K.S. Hegde Foundation Award for the year 1996

1997 Awarded Nikkei Asia Prize for Regional Growth by the Nikon Keizai Shimbun Inc. (NIKKEI), publisher of Japan's leading business daily

1996 Honorary Professor, Delhi School of Economics, University of Delhi, Delhi

1995 Jawaharlal Nehru Birth Centenary Award of the Indian Science Congress Association for 1994-95

1994	Asiamoney Award, Finance Minister of the Year
1994	Elected Distinguished Fellow, London School of Economics, Centre for Asia Economy, Politics and Society
1994	Elected Honorary Fellow, Nuffield College, University of Oxford, Oxford, U.K.
1993	Euromoney Award, Finance Minister of the Year
1993	Asiamoney Award, Finance Minister of the Year
1994	Honorary Fellow, All India Management Association
1987	**Padma Vibhushan Award** by the President of India
1986	National Fellow, National Institute of Education, N.C.E.R.T.
1985	Elected President, Indian Economic Association
1982	Elected Honorary Fellow, St. John's College, Cambridge, U.K.
1982	Elected Honorary Fellow, Indian Institute of Bankers
1976	Honorary Professor, Jawaharlal Nehru University, New Delhi
1957	Elected Wrenbury Scholar, University of Cambridge, U.K.

1955 Awarded Wright's Prize for distinguished performance, & St. John's College, Cambridge, U.K.

1956 Awarded Adam Smith Prize, University of Cambridge, U.K.

1954 Uttar Chand Kapur Medal, Panjab University, for standing first in M.A (Economics), Panjab University.

1952 University Medal for standing First in B.A. Hon. (Economics), Panjab University.

Recipient of Honorary Degrees of D.LITT. from:

- Panjab University, Chandigarh
- Guru Nanak University, Amritsar
- Delhi University, Delhi
- Sri Venkateswara University, Tirupathi
- University of Bologna, Italy
- University of Mysore, Mysore
- Chaudhary Charan Singh Haryana Agricultural University, Hisar (D.Sc)
- Kurukshetra University
- Thapar Institute of Engineering & Technology, Patiala (D.Sc)
- Nagarjuna University, Nagarjunanagar

- Osmania University, Hyderabad
- University of Roorkee, Roorkee (Doctor of Social Sciences)
- Doctor of Laws by the University of Alberta, Edmonton, Canada
- Dr. Bhimrao Ambedkar University (formerly Agra University) -Doctor of Letters degree
- Indian School of Mines, Dhanbad (Deemed University) D.Sc. (Honoris Causa)
- Pt. Ravishankar Shukla University, Raipur

Work Experience and Position Held

May 22, 2004 beacame	:	Prime Minister of India
Mar. 21, 1998-May 22, 04	:	Leader of Opposition, Rajya Sabha (Council of States) Parliament of India
June, 2001	:	Re-elected as Member of Rajya Sabha for a term of six years
Aug 1, 1996 - Dec 4, 1997	:	Chairman, Parliamentary Standing Committee on Commerce, Rajya Sabha
June 21, 1991-May 15, 1996	:	Finance Minister of India
June, 1995	:	Re-elected as Member of Rajya Sabha for a term of six years

September, 1991	:	Elected as a Member of Rajya Sabha
Mar 15, 1991- Jun 20, 1991	:	Chairman, University Grants Commission
Dec. 10, 1990-Mar 14, 1991	:	Adviser to Prime Minister of India on Economic Affairs
Aug. 1, 1987-Nov. 10, 1990	:	Secretary-General and Commissioner, South Commission
Jan. 15, 1985-July 31, 1987	:	Dy. Chairman, Planning Commission, India
Sept. 16, 1982-Jan. 14, 1985	:	Governor, Reserve Bank of India
April 1980 - Sept. 15, 1982	:	Member-Secretary, Planning Commission, India
Nov.1976 - April 1980	:	Secretary, Ministry of Finance, Dept. of Economic Affairs, Government of India Member for Finance, Atomic Energy Commission, Government of India Member for Finance, Space Commission, Government of India

1972 -1976	:	Chief Economic Adviser, Ministry of Finance, Government of India
1971 - 1972	:	Economic Adviser, Ministry of Foreign Trade, Government of India
1969- 1971	:	Professor of International Trade, Delhi School of Economics, Delhi University, India
1966 - 1969	:	UNCTAD, United Nations Secretariat, New York **1966-69** : Chief, Financing for Trade Section **1966** : Economic Affairs Officer
1957 - 1965	:	Panjab University, Chandigarh **1963-65** : Professor of Economics 1959-63: Reader in Economics **1957-59** Senior Lecturer in Economics

Other Assignments

Leader of the Indian delegation to the Commonwealth Heads of Government Meeting, Cyprus (1993)

Leader of the Indian delegation to the Human Rights World Conference, Vienna (1993)

Governor for India on the Board of Governors of the IMF and the International Bank for Reconstruction & Development (1991-95)

Appointed by Prime Minister of India as Member, Economic Advisory Council to the Prime Minister (1983-84)

Chairman, India Committee of the Indo-Japan Joint Study Committee (1980-83)

Leader, Indian Delegation to :

Indo-Soviet Monitoring Group Meeting (1982)

Indo-Soviet Joint Planning Group Meeting (1980-82)

Aid India Consortium Meetings (1977-79)

Member Indian Delegation to:

South-South Consultations, New Delhi (1982)

Cancun Summit on North-South Issues (1981)

Aid-India Consortium Meetings, Paris (1973-79)

Annual Meetings of IMF, IBRD & Commonwealth Finance Ministers (1972-79)

Third Session of UNCTAD, Santiago (April-May 1972)

Meetings of UNCTAD Trade & Development Board, Geneva (May 1971-July 1972)

Ministerial Meeting of Group of 77, Lima (October 1971)

Deputy for India on IMF Committee of Twenty on International Monetary Reform (1972-74)

Associate, Meetings of IMF Interim Committee and Joint Fund-Bank Development Committee (1976-80, 1982-85)

Alternate Governor for India, Board of Governors of IBRD - (1976-80)

Alternate Governor for India, Board of Governors of the IMF (1982-85)

Alternate Governor for India, Board of Governors, Asian Development Bank, Manila (1976-80)

Director, Reserve Bank of India (1976-80)

Director, Industrial Development Bank of India (1976-80)

Participated in Commonwealth Prime Ministers Meeting, Kingston (1975)

Represented Secretary-General UNCTAD at several inter-governmental meetings including:

Second Session of UNCTAD, 1968

Committee on Invisibles & Financing Related to Trade. Consultant to UNCTAD, ESCAP and Commonwealth Secretariat

Member, International Organizations:

Appointed as Member by the Secretary-General, United Nations of a Group of Eminent Persons to advise him on Financing for Development (December, 2000)

PUBLICATIONS

(i) Author of "*India's Export Trends and Prospects for Self-Sustained Growth*" published by Clarendon Press, Oxford University (1964).
(ii) Has published a large number of articles in economic journals

Addresses:

Office : South Block, New Delhi
Residence : 7, Race Course Road, New Delhi

Phones
(Off.) : 23012312,23013040, 23013067
(Resi.) : 23018939
Fax : 23017475, 23019334

CHAPTER

21

Manmohan's three Trouble Shooters at South Block

TKA Nair: Principal Secretary to the Prime Minister

TKA Nair

The first bureaucratic appointment made by Prime Minister Manmohan Singh shortly after assuming office was to induct his Chanakya, Mr. TKA Nair, as his Principal Secretary.

Mr. Nair has worked with Dr. Singh on several committees and the two are said to share an excellent equation. A 1963-batch

IAS officer of the Punjab Cadre, this is Mr. Nair's second innings at the PMO, the first being as part of Prime Minister I K Gujral's PMO in 1997-98. A former Chief Secretary of Punjab, Mr. Nair was the Chairman of the Public Enterprizes Selection Board before becoming Principal Secretary to Prime Minister Manmohan Singh.

Like Dr. Manmohan Singh, Mr. Nair was also an academician before joining the Government of India. He brings a wealth of experience to the PMO.

Mr. Nair was born and brought up in Kerala in a rural background.

He completed his schooling at the Government Primary School and the Christian High School in his native village, Ayroor. Mr. Nair did his post graduation at the University College, Trivandrum (Kerala). Before joining the IAS, he was a Lecturer in History and Political Science at St. Thomas College, and then at the Govt. College in north Kerala.

Mr. Nair cleared both the IAS and IFS examinations at the very first attempt but opted for the former. His first posting was as a Sub-Divisional Officer in Karnal. He went on to be Punjab's youngest DC, when posted at Hoshiarpur. He is still popular there because of the devlopment works he implemented in the district, and in view of his easy accessibility. Mr. Nair is known for his administrative and inter-personal skills.

He went to the University of Manchester for a three-year course in Public Administration. He served with the Punjab government in different capacities but it was in the field of industry that he made major contributions as Joint

Secretary, MD of Punjab Industrial Development Corporation and later as Principal Secretary.

Mr. Nair is recognized for his major contributions for furthering industrialization in Punjab and for facilitating the setting up of many industrial units in the state. Mr. Nair worked for five years as the Chairman of the Marine Products Exports Development Authority during which he brought prawn hatchery technology to India and also introduced value addition to this profession.

Mr. Nair had short stints in the Ministry of Rural Development at Additional Secretary level and in the Govt. of Punjab as Principal Secretary, Home Department. When he was Special Secretary in the Planning Commission, he was recalled by the Govt. of Punjab to serve as Chief Secretary. While he was Chief Secretary, the most peaceful Parliamentary elections (1996) were conducted in the state.

Mr. Nair returned to the Govt. of India in 1997 as Secretary in the Ministry of Environment and Forests. Selected in the PMO, he served as Secretary to the Prime Minister during the IK Gujral government and later, on retirement, moved to the Public Enterprises Selection Board as member, and thereafter, as Chairman. Streamlining the recruitment process, making it transparent and the introduction of new performance appraisal systems and models were some achievements during his tenure.

Mr. Nair has first hand experience of developmental works, and has expertise in setting up systems for empowering people to ensure self-sustaining growth.

JN Dixit: National Security Adviser

JN Dixit

JN Dixit, the National Security Adviser (NSA) in Dr. Manmohan Singh's government, has been given the rank of Minister of State. We can call Mr. Dixit as the modern -day Chanakya since he has great qualities of the master-strategist. Mr. Dixit is said to have been more powerful in the ten years after his retirement than he ever was during his service of thirty six years in the Indian Foreign Service (IFS). It is significant that Mr. Dixit's appointment as the NSA has received all-round welcome.

Mr. JN Dixit was educated in different parts of India as his parents were freedom fighters. He did his post-graduation in international law and international relations from Delhi. He later joined the Indian Foreign Service (IFS) in 1958, and retired in 1994 after a long and distinguished span of thirty-six years during which he served in different capacities in Indian embassies in South & North America, Japan and Western Europe. He also served at the headquarters of the Ministry of External Affairs.

His duty as India's chief diplomatic representative took him to Bangladesh, Afghanistan, Bhutan, Sri Lanka and Pakistan. He was also involved in assignments related to the United Nations (UN), SAARC and the Non-Aligned Movement. His career culminated in his elevation to the head of IFS from December 1991 to January 1994. His tenure as the Foreign Secretary witnessed - both in the national and international arenas - a series of dramatic, profound ad epoch-making events, which marked significant new directions. Many momentous happenings including the disintegration of the gigantic Soviet Union, the ethnic conflicts among the constituents of former Yugoslavia, the destruction of the Babri Masjid at Ayodhya, the Mumbai bomb blasts and, above all, the escalation of terrorism and violence in Jammu & Kashmir took place during his term in office. All these developments had international ramifications and repercussions, which also fell within the purview of the Indian Foreign Service.

Mr. JN Dixit joined the Congress Partry a year before the 2004 Lok Sabha elections, when the party was down in the dumps and political pundits did not visualize its early revival. He was appointed deputy to Mr. K. Natwar Singh, the External Affairs Minister, who was the Chairman of the party's Foreign Affairs Committee. He played a crucial role in formulating the party's agenda on defence, security and foreign policy before elections to the 14th Lok Sabha. On the issue of India's relations with the USA, the policy consistently held by Mr. Dixit is that the Indo-US relations should not be seen through the prism of a third country. The differences beteen India and Pakistan on the Kashmir issue should not come between the Indo-US ties. He is convinced that there are enormous possibilities of economic, strategic, technological and political co-operation on a wide range of subjects. He is also undeterred by the fears of increased Indo-US trade leading to India's economic colonisation. As National Security Adviser (NSA), Mr. Dixit's priorities are laid out clearly and he will have to focus on the many points like:

(i) Talks with Kashmir separatists and terrorism in Jammu & Kashmir,

(ii) Peace process with Pakistan,

(iii) Strategic partnership with the United States of America, and

(iv) Smooth relations with China, particularly the India-China talks on the boundary dispute.

But the most important (and covert) job of Mr. Dixit as NSA will be to ensure political stability.

MK Narayanan: Special Adviser to the Prime Minister

Former Intelligence Chief, also called 'Ace intelligence man', Mr. MK Narayanan is one more trouble shooter at South Block. is the Special Adviser to Prime Minister Dr. Manmohan Singh, with the rank of Minister of State.

Mr. Narayanan was the Chief of India's Intelligence Bureau (IB) in 1987-90, and after a brief break, he was brought back to head the IB in 1991. He has also been the Chairman of the Joint Intelligence Command. Mr. Narayanan was a member of panels set up to examine the recommendations of the Kargil Review Committee on Intelligence Structure and Internal Security.

He is seen as one of the most important links between 10 Janpath and the PMO, analysts say. He is known as one of the best intelligence brains in independent India. Mr. Narayanan took over his new challenging assignment on May 31, 2004, for a period of three years at South Block. Mr. Narayanan will act as Prime Minister Manmohan Singh's interface with all security outfits - including those of the Ministry of Home Affairs.

A Tamil Nadu cadre IPS officer of the 1955 batch, Mr. Narayanan had a long stint of 37 years in service. He will be advising the Prime Minister on such sensitive issues as talks with the Kashmiri organizations like the Hurriyat Conference, the functioning of intelligence agencies like the Intelligence Bureau (IB) and Research and Analysis Wing (RAW), and the handling of other issues related to internal security.

In this context, Mr. Narayanan he is expected to be 'one notch above' New Delhi's pointsmen in its talks with Kashmiri separatists. Mr. Narayanan has argued that India is facing terrorism and security challenges in Jammu & Kashmir, insurgency in North-East India, ethno-religious conflict in Gujarat, Madhya Pradesh (MP), Uttar Pradesh (UP), Orissa, Rajasthan, Andhra Pradesh and Bihar. He is also concerned about the growing organised crime in the urban areas in India.

CHAPTER

22

List of New Council of Ministers

CABINET MINISTERS

1. **Dr. Manmohan Singh**
   Prime Minister and also in-charge of the Ministries/ Departments not specifically allocated to the charge of any Minister viz..
   (i) Ministry of Personnel, Public Grievances & Pensions;
   (ii) Ministry of Planning;
   (iii) Department of Atomic Energy; and
   (iv) Department of Space.

2. **Shri Pranab Mukherjee**
Minister of Defence.

3. **Shri Arjun Singh**
Minister of Human Resource Development.

4. **Shri Sharad Pawar**
Minister of Agriculture and Minister of Consumer Affairs, Food & Public Distribution.

5. **Shri Lalu Prasad**
Minister of Railways.

6. **Shri Shivraj V. Patil**
Minister of Home Affairs.

7. **Shri Ram Vilas Paswan**
Minister of Chemicals & Fertilizers and Minister of Steel.

8. **Shri Ghulam Nabi Azad**
Minister of Parliamentary Affairs and Minister of Urban Development.

9. **Shri S. Jaipal Reddy**
Minister of Information & Broadcasting and Minister of Culture.

10. **Shri Sish Ram Ola**
Minister of Labour & Employment.

11. **Shri P. Chidambaram**
Minister of Finance.

12. **Shri Mahavir Prasad**
    Minister of Small Scale Industries and Minister of Agro & Rural Industries.

13. **Shri P.R. Kyndiah**
    Minister of Tribal Affairs and Minister of Development of North Eastern Region.

14. **Shri T.R. Baalu**
    Minister of Road Transport & Highways and Minister of Shipping.

15. **Shri Shankarsinh Vaghela**
    Minister of Textiles.

16. **Shri K. Natwar Singh**
    Minister of External Affairs.

17. **Shri Kamal Nath**
    Minister of Commerce & Industry.

18. **Shri H.R. Bhardwaj**
    Minister of Law & Justice.

19. **Shri P.M. Sayeed**
    Minister of Power.

20. **Shri Raghubansh Prasad Singh**
    Minister of Rural Development.

21. **Shri Priyaranjan Dasmunsi**
    Minister of Water Resources.

22. **Shri Mani Shankar Aiyar**
    Minister of Petroleum & Natural Gas and Minister of Panchayati Raj.

23. **Shri Sunil Dutt**
    Minister of Youth Affairs & Sports.

24. **Smt. Meira Kumar**
    Minister of Social Justice & Empowerment.

25. **Shri K. Chandra Shekhar Rao**
    Minister Without Portfolio.

26. **Shri Shibu Soren**
    Minister of Coal & Mines.

27. **Shri A. Raja**
    Minister of Environment & Forests.

28. **Shri Dayanidhi Maran**
    Minister of Communications & Information Technology.

29. **Dr. Anbumani Ramdoss**
    Minister of Health & Family Welfare.

MINISTERS OF STATE (INDEPENDENT CHARGE)

1. **Shri Santosh Mohan Dev**
   Minister of State (Independent Charge) of the Ministry of Heavy Industries & Public Enterprises.

2. **Shri Jagdish Tytler**
   Minister of State (Independent Charge) of the Ministry of Non-Resident Indians Affairs.

3. **Shri Oscar Fernandes**
Minister of State (Independent Charge) of the Ministry of Statistics & Programme Implementation.

4. **Smt. Renuka Chowdhury**
Minister of State (Independent Charge) of the Ministry of Tourism.

5. **Shri Subodh Kant Sahay**
Minister of State (Independent Charge) of the Ministry of Food Processing Industries.

6. **Shri Kapil Sibal**
Minister of State (Independent Charge) of the Ministry of Science & Technology and Minister of State (Independent Charge) of the Department of Ocean Development.

7. **Shri Vilas Muttemwar**
Minister of State (Independent Charge) of the Ministry of Non-Conventional Energy Sources

8. **Kumari Selja**
Minister of State (Independent Charge) of the Ministry of Urban Employment & Poverty Alleviation.

9. **Shri Praful Patel**
Minister of State (Independent Charge) of the Ministry of Civil Aviation.

10. **Shri Prem Chand Gupta**
Minister of State (Independent Charge) of the Ministry of Company Affairs.

MINISTERS OF STATE

1. **Shri E. Ahammed**
   Minister of State in the Ministry of External Affairs.

2. **Shri Suresh Pachauri**
   Minister of State in the Ministry of Personnel, Public Grievances & Pensions and Minister of State in the Ministry of Parliamentary Affairs.

3. **Shri B.K. Handique**
   Minister of State in the Ministry of Defence and Minister of State in the Ministry of Parliamentary Affairs.

4. **Smt. Panabaka Lakshmi**
   Minister of State in the Ministry of Health & Family Welfare.

5. **Dr. Dasari Narayan Rao**
   Minister of State in the Ministry of Coal & Mines.

6. **Dr. Shakeel Ahmad**
   Minister of State in the Ministry of Communications & Information Technology.

7. **Shri Rao Inderjit Singh**
   Minister of State in the Ministry of External Affairs.

8. **Shri Naranbhai Rathwa**
   Minister of State in the Ministry of Railways

9. **Shri K. Rehman Khan**
   Minister of State in the Ministry of Chemicals & Fertilizers.

10. Shri K.H. Muniappa
Minister of State in the Ministry of Road Transport & Highways.

11. Shri M.V. Rajasekharan
Minister of State in the Ministry of Planning.

12. Shri Kantilal Bhuria
Minister of State in the Ministry of Agriculture and Minister of State in the Ministry of Consumer Affairs, Food & Public Distribution.

13. Shri Manikrao Gavit
Minister of State in the Ministry of Home Affairs.

14. Shri Shriprakash Jaiswal
Minister of State in the Ministry of Home Affairs.

15. Shri Prithviraj Chavan
Minister of State in the Prime Minister's Office.

16. Shri Taslimuddin
Minister of State in the Ministry of Agriculture and Minister of State in the Ministry of Consumer Affairs, Food & Public Distribution.

17. Smt. Suryakanta Patil
Minister of State in the Ministry of Rural Development and Minister of State in the Ministry of Parliamentary Affairs.

18. Shri Md. Ali Ashraf Fatmi
Minister of State in the Ministry of Human Resource Development.

19. **Shri A. Narendra**
Minister of State in the Ministry of Rural Development.

20. **Shri R. Velu**
Minister of State in the Ministry of Railways.

21. **Shri S.S. Palanimanickam**
Minister of State in the Ministry of Finance.

22. **Shri S. Regupathy**
Minister of State in the Ministry of Home Affairs.

23. **Shri K. Venkatapathy**
Minister of State in the Ministry of Law & Justice

24. **Smt. Subbulakshmi Jagadeesan**
Minister of State in the Ministry of Social Justice & Empowerment.

25. **Shri E.V.K.S. Elangovan**
Minister of State in the Ministry of Commerce & Industry.

26. **Smt Kanti Singh**
Minister of State in the Ministry of Human Resource Development.

27. **Shri Namo Narain Meena**
Minister of State in the Ministry of Environment & Forests.

28. **Shri Jay Prakash Narayan Yadav**
Minister of State in the Ministry of Water Resources.

29. **Shri Akhilesh Singh**
Minister of State in the Ministry of Agriculture and Minister of State in the Ministry of Consumer Affairs, Food & Public Distribution.

Note: Incorporates changes in the Council of Ministers as on 25.05.2004.

Index